UN-FUNK YOURSELF

UN-FUNK YOURSELF

LEADING MINDFULLY IN THE MIDST OF MAYHEM

EMILY HAMPTON MORASH

First paperback edition: March 2025
Paperback: 978-1-955811-85-9
E-book: 978-1-955811-86-6
LCCN: 2024925319

Edited by Bryna Haynes and Paul Baillie-Lane
Cover design and layout by Bryna Haynes and Amy Salomone
Cover artwork by Tayisiya via AdobeStock
Author photo: Emily Morash

Published by WorldChangers Media
PO Box 83, Foster, RI 02825
www.WorldChangers.Media

LEADERS ARE SAYING ...

"*Un-Funk Yourself* is a game-changer for anyone looking to break free from the chains of self-doubt and recharge their leadership spark. Emily Hampton Morash has a gift for blending raw honesty with practical tools, making this book a refreshing and empowering read. With wit, wisdom, honesty, and a dash of tough love, she will take you on a journey of empowerment, overcoming self-imposed obstacles and moving forward. If you're ready to shake off the funk, then this is the book for you!" – **Jason Hawes, *New York Times* best-selling author, creator and star of the hit show *Ghost Hunters***

"*Un-Funk Yourself* is an essential read for leaders who seek to escape the traps of conventional, ego-driven leadership. In a conversational and direct tone, this book challenges readers to rethink their approach with a potent mix of practical advice, thought-provoking narratives, and pop culture references which make crucial aspects of leadership like mindfulness, emotional intelligence, and effective communication not only approachable but fun. This book is a must-read for anyone aspiring to cultivate a more impactful, authentic, and inclusive way of guiding their teams." **- Tim Hebert, CEO and Founder of Dirigo Leadership Consulting, author of *The Intentional Leader***

"In this book, author Emily Hampton Morash takes the reader on a journey to self-recognition and discovery that will help anyone who is open to growth. The book starts with a diagnosis that led the author to gain the insight that she needed to change, and to 'Un-funk' her own life that was fraught with anxiety. This necessary change helped Emily become an astute observer of human behavior—most especially leadership behavior. If you're ready for an honest and irreverent take on how to 'Un-funk' your own behavior and leadership style, then this is the book for you." – **Joe Abouzeid, 30-plus year media executive, Vice President, and General Manager, WIVB-TV/ WNLO CW23**

"Emily's ability to take complex, often highly nuanced, situations and feelings and make them relatable and understandable is an absolute gift. Her use of real language and situations takes mindfulness from a concept to an action." – **Jason Houck, Ecology Team Lead, Ardurra**

"I love *Un-Funk Yourself* by Emily Morash! It is a well-written business leadership book and also a road map on how to live a better life. It is written in a rare and wonderful manner that brings in humor and real-life experiences, and at times reads almost like a novel. I could not put it down. It is loaded with meaningful advice and her insight to people and situations is unique and refreshing. I have read lots of business leadership books, but have rarely been captivated the way I was by this one. Thank you, Emily." – **Dennis DiPrete, Principal, DiPrete Engineering**

CONTENTS

UN-FUNK YOURSELF

INTRODUCTION

I WAS ONLY FIFTEEN MINUTES into my presentation when I unceremoniously fell off the stage in front of a rather large audience.

My husband calls it my "Dave Grohl moment. Just not as cool."

How did it happen? Well, mostly it was because I wasn't made aware that there was a gap between the stage and the wall. There was no fluorescent tape, no railing, nothing to indicate that there was a foot-wide gap between the edge of the black stage and the wall. The carpet under the stage was also dark, and the stage lighting left the whole back area of the stage in shadow.

The result of this black-on-black setup was that, when I walked toward the giant projector screen to point out a very important chart, I fell right into the void.

Down I tumbled, falling three-feet-plus to the floor, and landed on the ball of my left foot. The rest of my body crashed down as my foot gave way.

I had never heard a stampede before that moment. A good portion of the 200-member audience ran toward the stage to help me. I felt hands grab me and pull me out from under the stage.

A woman asked, "Are you alright?"

"I don't know," I replied with complete honesty. The pain radiating from my foot was hot and cold at the same time. Clearly something was very wrong, but I had no idea what.

"Can you stand?" she asked.

I set my left toes down and the pain screamed up my foot and ankle. "Nope," I hissed. "I cannot stand."

A few people hoisted me back onto the stage where a very thoughtful someone removed my Dr. Martens boot so that the paramedics wouldn't have to cut it off. (Shout out to those boots for saving my ankle from breaking.) Another very thoughtful someone else held ice to my rapidly expanding foot while reassuring me that I was going to be okay.

With the mic still in my hand, I assured the crowd that I was doing fine, and offered to tell jokes while we waited for the paramedics to arrive. The mic battery died right after that. Divine intervention, I'm sure, as most of my jokes are unfit for professional audiences.

I was in pain, badly injured, 2,000 miles from home, and traveling alone.

But what was more interesting was what I *wasn't*. I wasn't embarrassed, angry, pouting, or scared. I wasn't fretting or freaking out. Rather, I was calm, present, observant, and still ready to tell bad jokes.

That, my friend, was no coincidence.

Of course, the situation was less than ideal. Should I have been warned about the gap between the stage and the wall? Ideally, yes. But ideals and reality rarely live in the same vicinity.

So, rather than being angry and ruminating on why the hell this happened to me and why it never should have happened and who was going to pay for this, I opted to focus on healing and strengthening my injured foot.

Turns out, I incurred a Lisfranc injury—a ligament tear and a shattered metatarsal—which required surgery, joint fusion, and nine weeks immobilized in a boot. Recovery takes twelve to eighteen months on average.

That one made me take a deep breath. But even as x-rays were being taken and pain meds were being administered, I was asking myself, "How can I see this as an opportunity?"

This would not have been the case a decade ago. Honestly, I don't even want to imagine how I would have managed (or, more accurately, failed to manage) that whole situation. But I do know that anger, self-pity, and fear would have been running rampant in my head, and probably busting out of my mouth, too.

See, I used to be an avid worrier. In most situations, I considered any and all what-ifs, prepping for the worst-case scenario and cataloging the myriad ways I could respond to whatever bullshit was about to go down. I spent an exorbitant amount of energy worrying about everything from money to the weather to illness to wild boars eating my family.

I was also preemptively defensive, short-fused, and smart-mouthed, always ready to intellectually duel someone should the need arise. And the need *always* arose. I made sure of that.

Sigh.

To top it all off, I was a total perfectionist. Everything in its place, perfectly symmetrical, neat and tidy. When it wasn't, I would obsess over it until I made myself sick. Like that time in college when I overslept and was nearly late for an exam. Halfway between my apartment and campus I had to pull over to vomit out the driver's side door because the stress of leaving my bed unmade was literally turning my stomach. I made it to class on time but could not focus because of the bed situation. I ended up breaking down in tears and asking my professor if I could please retake the exam because, "I just have to get home."

My professor, a typically cynical older man, told me that yes, I could retake the exam, but not before we discussed getting me some help for this anxiety issue. He then walked me to health services and sat with me until one of the nurses could see me.

Despite his kindness and the campus doctor's diagnosis, I refused to believe there was anything "wrong" with me. I was just a stressed-out college kid taking a full load of classes, working full time, and trying to have fun in the off time.

As a result, I remained angry, anxious, and obsessed for many more years.

Fast-forward to graduate school, during which my cohort met one weekend per month for two years. Each Sunday night, after the intensity of the Friday-to-Sunday schedule wound down, I would become violently ill. Regardless of how often or how loudly my body screamed at me that something was wrong, I doubled down on the need to be "perfect." I relentlessly drove myself to maintain an A average, work full time, and maintain my fractured marriage. "I'll be fine," I told myself. "I am fine. It's all *fine*." And the cycle would continue.

One Saturday night in September 2008, I experienced a veritable breakdown-slash-awakening while sitting cross-legged on my friend Scott's couch. With a beer in one hand

and the TV remote in the other as I searched for the Tennessee game, I realized that I had not sat down to drink a beer or watch my alma mater lose—I mean, play a game—in I didn't know how long. I hadn't stopped to breathe or enjoy a moment or just *be* in … years.

As I sat there, tears welling in my eyes and my breath catching in my throat, I looked at Scott and said, "I need to make a lot of changes. *Everything* needs to change."

Scott stared at me and said, "Is this because Tennessee is losing, or …?"

Good friends always know what to say.

As we stared at the TV, floating in a space of un-busyness and un-botheredness, the reality of my life crashed into my mind. I was working an underpaying, overtaxing job, living far away from family and friends whom I missed dearly, in a state I never, ever wanted to move to, languishing in a deteriorating marriage, driving a car I didn't choose, living in a home that I never wanted to buy. I was faking *my whole fucking life.*

I. Was. Not. Fine.

None of it was fine.

The only aspect of my life that wasn't fake was the loving bond I had with my sweet little boy, who more than anything needed his momma to be okay—and I was absolutely not okay.

That revelation launched an exploration of who I was and who I was not. I spent the next months and years discovering and unraveling the facades I'd adopted and unlearning all of the things I thought I should be doing. All along, I was, albeit unknowingly, journeying into *mindfulness.*

AWAKENING OUT OF THE FUNK

Awakenings are rarely pretty or smooth. Life transitions are challenging in general, but the practice of self-discovery amid life turmoil, especially when you've built a version of yourself using other people's expectations and playbooks, can be an excruciating and exhausting process. It's not like you can toss the fake version of yourself into the fires of Mount Doom and vanquish all the negative repercussions of inauthenticity in a single take. The earth doesn't just open up and swallow your fears, your anxieties, and your silly decisions in a single gulp. No, awakening into a new and better way of living is a continuous voyage through emotional processing, acceptance, and pivoting as life continues to happen around, with, and to you.

As I leaned, uncomfortably at first, into my authenticity and began setting boundaries and acknowledging flaws, I learned that the true me is pretty cool but also wildly misunderstood. And, if that was true for me, it stood to reason that a whole bunch of other cool people must feel the same way. Surely I couldn't be the only person who'd been plodding around the planet trying to be all things to all people while totally ignoring my true self and neglecting my real needs!

Then, about twelve years ago, my career shifted out of the nonprofit world and into workforce development and consulting. I quickly realized that the work I wanted to do—the work companies and municipalities needed—was much deeper than just SWOT analyses and strategic plans. Hyper-observing humans for my whole life has given me insight into predictable behavior patterns among people, especially on teams of all kinds, so that was where I decided to focus my research and training.

After years of going down psychology rabbit holes, interviewing hundreds of leaders, and working with countless teams in numerous companies, The Mindful Leader Practice (the workshop that inspired this book) was born. The book you're reading followed about five years later.

So, here I am, Emily Hampton Morash, fearless falleroffer of stages and staunch advocate for mindfulness in all aspects of life, business, and leadership, speaking to you from the pages of a book—which was the last thing on Earth I ever saw myself doing.

I'm not anyone special, really. I'm not a PhD, an MD, or any other "D." I can't diagnose you or give you a prescription. I can't even juggle. But I am a human who has journeyed to my own personal Mordor flanked by people who supported me, battled my inner Orcs, learned an enormous amount about human behavior and the art of becoming mindful, and then shared my insights with tens of thousands of leaders all over the world.

This book was born from my journey into self-awareness, and it's intentionally both totally irreverent and as real as you can get. It's also based in real, measurable results, hard science, and a boatload of direct experience. I don't take myself seriously, but I take my mission to un-funk the leadership world very, very seriously.

So, if you prefer your authors to be on the pretentious and authoritative side, hate reading relatable stories about real people and teams who un-funked their leadership and communication skills, or are averse to occasional cuss words, this is probably not the book for you. But if you're tired of the theories and want real answers and actionable practices, and also enjoy bad metaphors, heavy metal, and *Star Trek* references, you will absolutely want to keep reading.

What I have learned is that leaders like you are the culture creators, the changemakers, and the stage-setters for not only your immediate team but for everyone in your orbit. And, it's highly possible that you don't even know it. So many leaders do not understand how important they are in the greater workforce ecosystem, or how far and wide the ripples of their behaviors reach. They can impact people mindfully and in a positive way through small, everyday actions, and they can also do deep, sometimes irreversible damage when they act and react in a mindless way.

The truth is, most people are what I called "funked up." We're messy messes of emotions and fears wrapped around a need and desire to be accepted, which in turn fuels those emotions and fears. When we don't know this is happening, or why it happens, the mess seeps into our behaviors at work, at home, and out in the community.

This may sound icky and a little depressing, but actually, it's great news. I've seen again and again how, when the reasons for our "messy" are illuminated and we gain insight into our own minds, needs, patterns, emotions, assumptions, judgments, and biases, things actually start to look brighter for us. We have context for the stuff that used to hit us out of nowhere, and can begin to work with those messy bits in a loving, non-judgmental way almost immediately.

If every leader in every company paused just a bit to do self-awareness work, our workplaces would be much more effective, productive, and profitable.

Don't believe me? Trust me, by the time you finish reading this book, you'll understand.

MORE STUFF YOU NEED TO KNOW

I was diagnosed with ADHD at the age of forty-two. As the evaluator and I pored through the results of my assessment, my brain started spinning around my various life experiences. Holy crap! It all made so much sense!

We spent most of our time exploring how the H presents for me. My H is hyper-observance. I notice everything, feel my emotions intensely, and have an insecurity-based chameleon style (aka, masking) so that I can connect and engage with others. I am hyper-curious with an insatiable desire to learn and a propensity to become easily overwhelmed. I give Charlie Kelly vibes when I gather and link information, especially when it relates to human behavior. I am also an intuitive, sensitive empath, picking up on others' emotions and motives even if they're trying to suppress them. If I don't keep tabs on myself, this combination of superpowers can shut me down for days.

After processing this info for a good minute, I recognized that I had to learn how to manage my brain. I was not interested in meds (my body is persnickety about medications), but I was curious about other methods of management—which is how I began my journey into meditation and yoga.

Both of the above—meditation and yoga—have become buzzwordy punchlines, especially in some workspaces, but at their genuine, not-an-influencer-trying-to-sell-you-something core, they are powerful tools of self-awareness and self-management. When I started using them regularly, I realized that I had never felt so good before. I was clear-headed, light-hearted, and unburdened by what before had seemed daunting and heavy.

Sprinkled throughout this book are links to guided

meditations and affirmations that you may find handy as you embark on this journey. You can find all of the resources mentioned in this book at **unfunkyourselfbook.com**.

When you come across a topic that feels heavy—and you will—please stop at that point and explore the heaviness. The meditations and resources on the above website will help you unpack the feelings mindfully and become okay with moving through them.

In addition to the meditations, you'll also find loads of journal prompts to work with, both in the book itself and on my website at **unfunkyourselfbook.com**. I highly encourage you to use these to the fullest possible extent as you meander through your mindfulness journey. And meander you should. This is not a race. You can't speed-run mindfulness because there is no fixed destination. Just like life itself, mindfulness is a fluid, ever-changing journey. But that doesn't mean that, with a little time and effort, you won't find yourself surrounded by a much more inviting landscape.

You also don't need to do this alone. None of us are alone in our messy funked-upness, so why should we be alone in our mindfulness? If you want to spend time with other leaders who are committed to learning mindfulness the no-drama-llama way, join the community on Instagram at **@unfunk_yourself_book**.

My dream for you is that, by the time you finish reading this book, you will know yourself on a different level than you have before. I'll bet that you, too, are pretty cool and also wildly misunderstood—and I can't wait to learn more about you.

And, if you really sit with what you're about to learn, do the journaling, practice the meditations, and be loving and patient with yourself, your life and leadership will begin to change in a positive way.

Soon, you too may be mindful enough to keep a smile on your face when you careen off the back of an unmarked stage—but I hope, for your sake, that you are also present enough to mind the gap.

Shall we proceed?

CHAPTER ONE

BAD BOSSES, GOOD INTENTIONS

"YOU STUPID BITCH!"

I barely had time to register what was happening as Miranda stormed into my office, slamming the door against the wall as she entered.

I stood up, phone receiver in hand, and said calmly to the donor on the line, "May I call you back, please?"

"How *dare* you!" Miranda screeched. And then, she threw her cell phone directly at my head.

I ducked, letting the phone sail past my shoulder and into the wall behind me. "What the hell, Miranda?"

She aimed her keys at my torso next and let fly. When I dodged again, she flew into a rage, knocking everything off my dcsk and onto the floor.

"What are you doing?" I yelled, horrified.

"You asked the Women's Garden Club to sponsor the employment program! Did that give you some sort of sick satisfaction?"

"What?"

"Satisfaction. They *rejected* my membership! I'm not good enough to be in their little sorority, but *you* are?"

I took a deep breath. "I'm not a member of the Women's Garden Club, nor have I applied to be. I was also not aware that *you'd* applied to be. So, I have no idea what you're talking about."

"Oh, you must be so *proud* of yourself," she seethed, looking around for something else to hit. I moved back behind my desk, trying to keep the furniture between us. "We are not taking their money. In fact, you will never ask those snotty bitches for *anything. Ever. Again.*"

"Miranda, we need to raise $50,000 a year for this program to function, and they've agreed to a multi-year partnership. They're guaranteeing $10,000 a year."

"We're not taking their money. Find it somewhere else, or find another job. Now, give me my phone and keys."

I bent down to pick up the phone. Its screen was spider-webbed from the impact. I placed it and the keys on my desk within her reach, and retreated again.

She raised her eyes slowly to mine. She was literally shaking with hatred. "Get out of my sight, Emily. *I do not trust you.*"

Never mind that this was, in fact, my office.

I left as fast as I could. The woman was obviously rabid. Totally unhinged.

Holy shit.

I'd been hired seven months prior to develop and direct a large, multipurpose revenue generation program for this non-profit. My job was to interface with donors, oversee workforce development training, and provide part-time employment for residents of the housing program.

I learned quickly that Miranda had a temper and was feared by most of the staff. She often remarked that new hires were put on a short leash—but she had a "good feeling" about me.

"How comfortable are you with disciplinary conversations?" she asked during one of our supervisory meetings about three months into my job. I replied that they weren't my favorite, but I was fairly comfortable with them. Soon after, I was asked to conduct discipline conversations for people who were not on my team. I was also asked to assist HR with termination conversations.

"She calls you her henchman," Erin, the HR assistant, told me over lunch one day. "You're better at this stuff than she is, honestly. She usually yells at people."

So, basically, I was doing her job? I wasn't okay with that.

During my next supervision conversation with Miranda, I expressed my discomfort related to leading discipline conversations for employees who weren't on my team. I wondered if this might constitute a breach of confidentiality.

"So, you think I'm unethical?" she asked.

"No, I'm just saying that it feels inappropriate for me to be conducting these conversations with people who don't report to me and whose results don't fall under my umbrella of responsibility."

"I see." She paused, and then put on a sneer. "Well, it seems like you're not interested in being a team player for this agency. As a director, you're expected to assist with operations, including redirecting employees. Erin and Lana don't directly oversee people, and they have these conversations. So, you can, too."

"Erin and Lana are HR," I clarified.

Her eyes slitted. "You're a director. Do your damn job."

She canceled our supervision meetings for a few weeks after that.

When we finally met again the following month, she informed me that two managers involved in my program were not performing adequately. According to her, I needed to issue verbal warnings and a thirty-day performance improvement plan to each of them, because a few of the social workers were complaining that they were acting inappropriately and wasting agency dollars.

"Who is complaining?" I'll get specifics from them so I can investigate and figure out next steps."

"Oh, no, don't do that. They don't report to you, so it would be *inappropriate* for you to talk with them, now wouldn't it?"

"But—"

"If you don't have the balls to write up your managers, I'll do it for you."

"I am plenty capable, thank you, but I can't issue warnings without actual evidence of poor behavior."

"Maybe if you paid more attention to your staff, you wouldn't have to get info secondhand. In fact, if you were paying attention, we wouldn't even be *having* this conversation. Maybe *you're* the one who needs a warning and an improvement plan."

Two weeks after that conversation, she crashed into my office and broke her phone on my wall. Once she'd cleared out, I grabbed my stuff and walked out the door. She officially fired me two days later as a "no show."

Miranda wasn't my first Bad Boss. But she definitely took home the award for "Baddest Boss Ever."

***

After that experience, I thought I was crystal clear about how *not* to manage people. Sadly, it took me quite a bit longer to understand that good bosses don't manage people, we *lead* them. In fact, it wasn't until a few years later, when I had my own experience of being a Bad Boss, that I realized I had no idea how to actually lead people.

Here's what went down.

Kara was an incredibly talented fundraiser, responsible for the largest and highest-grossing walk event in our region. She was brilliant, creative, persuasive, and a strategic negotiator. She was also young and—in my not-so-humble opinion—professionally green.

I conducted weekly supervision meetings with all members of my team. There were many proverbial balls in the air, especially during event season, and all of us needed to be on the same page.

"I think these meetings are a waste of time," Kara expressed one morning. "Everything you need to know, everything we cover in these check-ins, is already in the system."

"Yes, but the meetings give us a chance to connect and brainstorm any challenges you're having," I replied.

"I appreciate that, but I don't need to connect, and I am not having any challenges. Whenever I have challenges, I bring them up in the moment. I don't wait until a scheduled meeting."

"Well..." I paused, taken aback. "You have yet to secure a presenting sponsor for your event, and we need to determine who that's going to be and how we're going to approach them."

"Actually, there are two companies interested in being the presenting sponsor. One may be better suited for the entertainment sponsor, so I'm walking through the benefits of each with both companies tomorrow."

"Why didn't you tell me this? Why am I not involved in the sponsor conversations?"

"Like I said, all the information is in the system. All my notes are up to date. I don't need to involve you because I am already working with these companies. You don't need to hold my hand, Emily."

My hackles went *way* up. "You are not communicating with me, and you're withholding information. That's unacceptable."

Immediately after Kara left my office, I called HR for guidance on issuing a warning for insubordination. I explained my interpretation of what happened, and my HR liaison provided information on how to issue and record the warning.

The following morning, I informed Kara that she was receiving a verbal warning for insubordination and that, should she continue to omit communication, she would receive a written warning.

She looked at me for what felt like a long time, then muttered, "Okay."

"*Okay*? That's all you have to say?"

"There isn't anything else *to* say. This is ridiculous. Everything you need to know is in the system that we're required to use—the one you pull reports from daily. I am not withholding information. You're just not looking at it."

Oh, snap.

"You need to change your attitude," I huffed.

The following Monday, I was greeted by Kara's resignation letter, effective immediately. She was taking her talents, and her connections, to another large nonprofit.

This was my fault. *I* did this. All because I couldn't keep my reactions in check and see things from Kara's point of view.

THE BALLAD OF THE FUNKED-UP BOSS

What I've shared above are just two examples of, shall we say, less than stellar leadership. Miranda, of course, is an extreme example. She was explicitly abusive, totally reactive, and basically tyrannical—the kind of Bad Boss featured in novels, blockbuster movies, and work-related nightmares.

Miranda presented with some pretty unhinged behaviors: deep levels of passive aggression, threats, physical abuse, emotional manipulation, triangulation, and losing her ever-loving mind over what she perceived to be competition for status. She ruled by fear and used trust and relationships as weapons to maintain control.

If you have a boss like Miranda, my advice is to get the hell out, now, and fire off some exposé-style reports to HR on your way out.

But the second example? It's also toxic, just more subdued. This is the kind of poor leadership that we all have experienced—and maybe even perpetuated—in the workplace.

Knowing what I know now, I cringe at my Bad Boss moment. But I've also learned to lean into compassion for the version of me who thought she had to micromanage to maintain control. I wasn't a bad person. I was just a bit … funked up.

Like I said, Kara was a phenomenally talented fundraiser, able to secure millions of dollars in a short period of time. She was also fresh out of college and lacked the ability to navigate team dynamics, see the big picture, and learn a more holistic approach to her job. This was my observation, and it was true. But she also lacked a strong leader to guide her and impart some wisdom around visionary thinking and strategy with regard to the partnerships she was building. I was meant to be that leader, but I hadn't yet learned how to lead. I only knew how to manage.

I wasn't a great communicator, either, so I wasn't able to objectively course-correct when she presented her point of view. In that moment, it was my way or the highway. I mindlessly moved and reacted from ego and my own fear of judgment. I assumed she didn't see me as talented, valuable, or important. I was offended that she didn't want to connect and brainstorm, and that she didn't come to my office to share exciting news about potential sponsors. I was insulted by her flippancy when I "corrected" her. I was just pissed off at the whole situation, because *why didn't she like me?*

Well, I found out later that she did like me. Right up until that moment when I lost my shit and funked up the entire conversation.

Social media philosophers often state that people don't leave bad jobs, they leave Bad Bosses. *Preach*, internet meme makers! This is totally on point, and I'm about to show you why.

First, leaders are a bit like teachers. Everyone can learn to be one, but not everyone wants to be one, and not everyone should be one. Truly Bad Bosses (notice the capital B's) are just that: bad. They behave poorly, to say the very least, and have absolutely no interest in improving their emotional intelligence or changing their style—because, in their minds, *they're* not wrong, everyone else is. They believe that power is finite, and that being loud, crude, abusive, demeaning, and condescending is the best way to hold on to their piece of the power pie.

In short, Bad Bosses don't give a shit if they're bad or not. So, I'm going to guess that you, dear reader, are not actually a Bad Boss. (Miranda is definitely *not* reading this book.) What's more, truly Bad Bosses are, if not rare, at least not common.

But if you're not a Bad Boss, why does leadership feel so hard, and why do you keep making mistakes, getting triggered, and spinning your wheels?

It's because, like me, you're a little funked up.

And, since this is a book about how to "un-funk" your leadership, you are absolutely in the right place.

Every decent boss has a few bad moments here and there. Many even have a terrible approach to one particular aspect of leadership—like providing feedback, managing conflict, or talking with people who they find intimidating—but that doesn't make them Bad Bosses. Having a bad moment doesn't make you, me, or anyone a bad person.

Like most people, I learned my managerial style from some really awful bosses who did a great job of teaching me what *not* to do. (Note, names have been changed to protect the no-so-innocent and likely litigious.)

For example, there was Liza, who openly gossiped—like during the holiday potluck when, in front of the whole staff, she wondered, loudly, if one of her young female employees "charges by the hour in that dress."

Then, there was Derek, who repeatedly stole his employees' ideas—like that time when he presented my plan to upper management and took all the credit for what would eventually become a national organizational campaign.

Then, there was Molly, who outright refused to in-person train people she didn't like. She provided only written instructions, gaslit them when they asked for further clarification, and said things like, "We covered this in the meeting. You should be taking notes." When they didn't understand their roles, she wrote them up and fired them for incompetence.

Sadly, I can think of only one boss in my career whose behavior was a model for good leadership (thank you, Heidi!), and I only worked with her for a few years. The result was that I didn't have much to go on. Maybe you don't either.

When good people step into Bad Boss territory, it's often a case of misalignment. We feel funky (not the good, groovy kind, but the something-is-wrong-and-I'm-weirded-out kind). In other words, we're misaligned, disengaged, disconnected, overwhelmed, undermotivated, and sometimes just plain having a crappy day. We're stuck in our emotional brains, struggling to see the light of logic through the fog of our feelings. And then, someone comes along and pushes *just the right button* to launch us into full reactor mode or send us scurrying under our desks.

Human beings are emotional before we are logical. It's how we are wired. This is true no matter how smart, accomplished, or "in control" we are. We unconsciously rely heavily on our primal brain—the amygdala specifically—to determine if a person or situation is safe or a threat. And, since our amygdala is where fight/flight and the memories associated with previous fight/flight moments sit, it perceives emotional stress the same way it perceives physical threat.

Yes, your brain will perceive a nasty email or a flippant reply from a key employee with the exact same stress response as it does a steep cliff, a charging bear, or a thrown cell phone. We are hardwired to react in those moments to preserve life and limb. As Brené Brown famously described it, "Thinking and behavior are hog-tied in the back, and emotion is driving like a bat out of hell."

When we're feeling funky, we're exponentially more likely to react rather than to respond. This means that, in challenging moments, we are more often than not reacting from emotional interpretations of what we perceive is happening, rooted in past experiences and the fears and judgments associated with them. In those moments, all our best intentions and logical training goes out the window. We want to do the right thing, but the right thing just isn't accessible.

Here are just a few examples from my own working life to demonstrate how this funked-up leadership can look.

- Martin doesn't do one-to-one check-ins. He tells his staff that "no news is good news," and jokes that if he ever asks for a check-in, they should be worried.
- David prefers to placate. He tells his employees that they're "doing a great job" and feels that goal setting is too stressful.
- Helen hates conflict, so she never provides course-correction feedback in real time. Instead, she waits until semi-annual evaluations to ding employees' performance, issue improvement plans, and/or withhold merit increases. Her team members are often taken completely by surprise by their negative performance reviews.

- Jane is indecisive, delaying decision-making until someone else brings it up and often changing her mind under the slightest pressure.
- Carl has a tough time with accountability and often blames his employees when things go wrong.

What all these folks have in common, besides irritated employees and some challenging internal conflict, is a lack of mindfulness. The bosses I've described above are disconnected and disengaged, not just from their true roles as leaders, but also from others in their circles and from themselves. The result? No one gets what they need to do their best work every day.

THE TRUE COST OF FUNKED-UP LEADERSHIP

No one is deliberately "mindless," but most people were never taught to function mindfully. Furthermore, they may think that "mindfulness" is a heap of woo-woo bullshit for hippies and those yoga people. (Hard pass on the patchouli, thanks.)

And as for *leading* mindfully ... well, we're definitely not taught that. We just pick things up along the way from our own bosses, as well as our personal upbringing, culture, and social groups. Many times, the boss behavior that has been modeled to us—especially those of us who are Millennials, Gen-Xers, or Baby Boomers—is a do-as-I-say-not-as-I-do, my-way-or-the-highway approach. In modern, diverse workplaces, these attitudes simply do not fly anymore.

There's a heavy cost associated with bad leadership, and it goes way beyond grumpy employees, water-cooler complaining, employee turnover, or bad reviews on Glassdoor. There are tangible, measurable, and multifaceted emotional, health, and financial costs to funked-up leadership that are, quite frankly, terrifying to anyone who genuinely cares about the success of their team and organization.

For example, ineffective leadership is highly correlated with a loss in productivity. This can show up as time away from work, such as increased absenteeism, sick leave, stress leave, and eventual turnover. But when employees do show up, the effects continue. Recent research suggests that, in general, employees waste between 10 and 52 percent of their time at work withdrawing, avoiding, networking for support, and ruminating about their situation.

Also, according to an article published in the *Harvard Business Review*:

- 48 percent intentionally decreased their work effort.
- 38 percent intentionally decreased the quality of their work.
- 63 percent lost work time avoiding the boss.
- 78 percent said that their commitment to the organization declined.
- 25 percent admitted to taking their frustration out on customers.[(1)]

---

(1) Christine Porath, Christine Pearson. "The Price of Incivility." *Harvard Business Review*, Jan-Feb 2013. https://hbr.org/2013/01/the-price-of-incivility

Let's do some mathing.

According to TrainingIndustry.com, if we calculate a rough estimate of time wasted at work and time out of work, we could easily reach $75,000 per report. Estimate that every boss has at least five reports and you have a conservative loss of $375,000 per year per funked-up leader.

And, we haven't even looked at the emotional and health costs related to the stress that funked-up leadership causes.

Here are some tip-of-the-iceberg numbers from the Occupational Safety and Health Administration (OSHA):

- 83 percent of U.S. workers suffer from work-related stress.
- U.S. businesses lose up to $300 billion yearly because of workplace stress.
- Stress causes around one million workers to miss work every single day.
- Only 43 percent of US employees think their employers care about their work-life balance.
- Depression leads to $51 billion in costs due to absenteeism and $26 billion in treatment costs.
- Work-related stress causes 120,000 deaths and results in $190 billion in healthcare costs yearly.[(2)]

And guess what? Those numbers don't just include people at the bottom of the corporate ladder. Bosses are part of those

(2) "Workplace Stress." Occupational Safety and Health Administration. https://www.osha.gov/workplace-stress

statistics, too. Funked-up leadership affects *everyone.*

You know the old saying: happy employees are productive employees. The opposite is also true. And, while everyone has their own personal funk going on both at work and outside of office hours, employees are made measurably happier or unhappier by the culture in which they work—and that culture is set by their bosses.

Leaders are like the kidneys of the organizational body in that they are designed to help filter out toxins. If you have a super toxic person on your team and you, as the boss, allow the behavior, you're not doing your job as a kidney. And, if you've ever had a kidney stone, you'll know that the longer you ignore it, the more painful it is when it's time to remove it. Mindful leadership is the best preventative medicine.

Let's be honest: no one, including you, wants to work in a negative environment in which lack of trust, miscommunication, and unhealthy conflict are present. A workplace like that drains everyone's energy, including yours, and leads to low morale, low productivity, and gigantic monetary losses. And, since we don't live any part of our lives in a vacuum, our stress spills over into our home lives, and suffering abounds.

ARE YOU FUNKED UP? THE QUIZ

The discussion we've had in this chapter is not designed to accuse you of Bad Bossery. Nor is it my intention to make you feel guilty or imply in any way that you're not cut out to be a leader. (If you read it that way, now's a good time to take a deep breath and check in with that amygdala. What fight-or-flight buttons did I push back there?)

Rather, I've started this book in this way because I want to shake you up enough to truly see the cost of funked-up leadership, and to take a real, objective look at the state of your team, your organization, and your own inner world.

Bottom line is, all of us, no matter what our roles at work, at home, or in the community, are morally obligated to un-funk ourselves. Short-circuiting our reactions and approaching tough situations with grace is literally the best and fastest way to improve all aspects of our lives, relationships, and success outcomes. As a leader, doing this work is even more urgent because everything you do (or don't do) has an immediate and powerful ripple effect.

You're probably wondering at this point, "How am I supposed to know if I'm a funked-up boss?"

Well, lucky for you, I have a handy list of questions for you to ponder.

But before you just skim over them … stop.

Take a deep breath in, all the way to the top of your lungs.

Now, hold that breath for two seconds.

Now, exhale with force, and do all of the above again.

(Now that you're calm, please proceed.)

Remember that there is no judgment needed. You are a good person with good intentions, as evidenced by the fact that you're reading this book. You also may just happen to have some funky leadership habits—which, like all unhelpful habits, can be corrected with practice, attention, and mindfulness. So, I invite you to view this as an opportunity to learn and grow, not to condemn or shame yourself or anyone else.

Slowly read the following questions and pay attention to how the words hit your mind and how they make you feel (comfortable, uncomfortable). Make note of where you feel sensations in your body (I'll explain this in detail later in the book). Again, no matter how you answer, there's no judgment. We're all about finding solutions.

Is Your Leadership Funked Up?

Answer yes or no to the following statements:

1. I partake in or allow gossip in the workplace.
2. Bottom line numbers feel more vital to me than employee well-being.
3. I distrust one or more of my staff.
4. I feel like I don't really belong in a leadership role.
5. I feel like I need to prove my worth.
6. If someone doesn't do the task correctly, I just step in and do it.
7. I need my employees to like me.
8. I prefer email or chats to in-person conversations.
9. There is a lot of turnover on my team.
10. I have a favorite employee.
11. I believe kindness is a weakness in leadership.
12. In my company, we do things the way they've always been done.
13. I am the boss, so I call the shots.

14. I don't hire people who I perceive as being smarter than me.

15. I avoid conflict and tough conversations.

16. Feedback is only from me to my employees.

17. I worry that employees will take advantage of me.

18. My colleagues annoy me.

19. I'm only here for the paycheck and the pension.

20. I don't regularly praise my employees' good work.

If you answered "yes" to one or more of these, you have some funk happening in your leadership approach.

You're not funky on purpose. You're not malevolent. You're not lazy. You just never received the guidance you needed to be an un-funked leader.

Over the years I have met and coached hundreds of seasoned and emerging leaders, most of whom were funky in at least one of the areas listed above. Many enjoyed directing teams but struggled with many or all facets of leading; namely, conflict mediation, redirection, and setting expectations. Without exception, those who applied the techniques I'm about to teach you in this book radically improved their leadership and overall outcomes.

In other words, this stuff works. For real.

MINDFULNESS IS THE GREAT UN-FUNKIFIER

The ripple effects of mindlessness are infinite, and so are the ripple effects of mindfulness. The great news is, mindfulness is a skill that anyone can learn, and it will have benefits across all areas of your life.

And here's what's really cool about being mindful. As you become more mindful as a leader, those around you will tend to do so as well. You will model this brilliant manner of approaching work, discussions, and relationships for the folks who report to you, and they will absorb it and imitate it.

Before we dive into what mindfulness is (and isn't), let's learn a bit about the human brain and the physiology of the brain/mind connection.

As we learned above, we humans have developed *lots* of processing power and intellectual capacity as we've evolved, but the reality is that we are still ruled by our primal brain—our *emotional* brain, and specifically by the amygdala.

Emotions and their management are key components to what I call the Leadership Secret Sauce.

(Yeah, baby. I'm talking about *emotions* in a leadership book. And if you just had a moment of judgment there about what does and doesn't belong in a business book, you might just be in the throes of an *emotional* reaction. But I digress.)

Let's get nerdy for a second. The amygdala is an almond-shaped structure located in the temporal lobe. It is diverse and complex in structure and comprises approximately thirteen nuclei—which is to say, it's *really* small—but it has a gigantic job. It's a major processing center for emotions as well as a neural liaison to many other brain abilities, especially memories, learning, and your five senses. This is the part of your brain in which emotional memory and fight/flight reside, and its job is to resource past experiences to alert you to potentially scary and dangerous situations.

Our species would not have survived were it not for the mighty amygdala, and it continues to serve an important function. But when we exist in our emotional brain as a rule or allow it to override our "higher" brain in important moments, we suffer misunderstandings, miscommunication, and misjudgments. There is an inverse relationship between the emotional brain, where the amygdala lives, and the logical brain, where our executive functioning sits. The more activated the primal brain, the less active the logical brain. We're not trying to negotiate in a fight/flight/freeze situation; we're trying to survive.

Additionally, the amygdala doesn't work like an on/off switch. It's more like a dimmer switch. Some experiences, like navigating light traffic, switch on the amygdala just a little bit—like mood lighting for your commute, only not sexy—but being cut off on the highway by someone who then slams on their brakes and nearly causes an accident can make that dimmer switch shoot up to eleven. You've probably experienced both, so you know that when that person cut you off, you didn't start reasoning, "Maybe they're late to a meeting? Or perhaps someone is ill and this person needs to get home urgently?" No, you likely slammed on your brakes as hard as you could and yelled "*Asshole!*" at the top of your lungs. Maybe you added some nifty hand gestures for emphasis.

Not a whole lot of "logical" going on there, my friend.

Developing and practicing mindfulness is imperative to

learning to work with the amygdala, because mindfulness generates self-reflection. When you're paying attention to yourself, how you feel, and why you're feeling that way, you will begin to recognize when your amygdala is being triggered. You can then make decisions that are more in line with your actual goals, and as a result, create more positive outcomes.

So, one simple definition of mindfulness could be, "Paying attention to my mind."

Jon Kabat-Zinn, Professor Emeritus of medicine and the creator of the Center for Mindfulness in Medicine, Health Care, and Society at the University of Massachusetts Medical School, defines mindfulness as "awareness that arises through paying attention, on purpose, in the present moment, non-judgmentally."(3)

"Awareness that arises" isn't the surface observation we so often take as truth. Such observations are often clouded by—you guessed it—our emotions. The truth is under the surface. Allowing it to rise requires patience and intention. A great example of this is the difference between what I "knew" to be true in the moment I delivered the verbal warning to Kara—namely that she was being insubordinate and disrespectful—and what I realized later, which was that I felt unliked and invalidated by her perspective and wanted to push back.

Paying attention on purpose is not something that human beings do well naturally. By design, we are reactive to our surroundings. Without mindfulness to temper this tendency, we are consistently, persistently distracted by and reactive to everything around us.

(3) https://ed.buffalo.edu/mindful-assessment/scale/domains/mindful-awareness.html

Don't believe me? Next time you're out and about, notice how often you shift your eyes to take in your surroundings. Notice how you get pulled out of conversation by sparkly things, squirrels, or people you're judging. And ... where's your cell phone right now? Are you checking your socials between paragraphs of this chapter? Are you reading this with the TV on? If you are, it's okay. Humans crave distraction. Distraction, however, is dangerous when it collides with the distractions and emotions of other humans in our everyday relationships.

Being "present" and allowing awareness to arise means we're not worrying about the future or ruminating about the past. We're not assigning opinions or judgments to what's happening, not even to our own thoughts. (Honestly, this is the hardest part of the whole practice, but it's possible). We are simply here, now, allowing whatever is unfolding to just ... be.

For a day—or just an hour—could you stop forming snap judgments about people and situations? Be okay with uncertainty or not knowing the answer right this very second? Stop making assumptions and patiently seek out the truth instead?

If the answer is no, then guess what: you are exactly like 99 percent of other humans on this planet.

If you're wondering what the heck this all has to do with leadership, I'll tell you.

Everything. It has *everything* to do with leadership, work culture, relationships, and every other metric of success that gets debated over the boardroom table. If you cannot be present to what is happening in front of you and respond from that awareness, you will not be leading from a place of truth. You will be leading from your hijacked emotional brain. And, trust me when I tell you, no good decisions get made there. Your amygdala doesn't give a shit about your goals. It only wants to feel safe. Right. Now. (Bat out of hell, remember?)

Un-funking your leadership happens naturally when you put mindfulness to work at work. You'll learn a lot in this book about your brain, emotional intelligence, communication styles, and so much more. But underneath it all will be this concept of mindfulness. None of the other stuff works if you're not present and paying attention.

So, I invite you to do some light mental analysis over the next few days. The next time you're out to dinner, in the pickup line at your kids' school, or waiting in line at the coffee shop, notice how many times you assess a total stranger and create an assumption about them. More, notice what you believe this assumption says about *you*. Then, take a deep breath, and ask yourself, "What am I not seeing here?" I promise, some of what you learn will blow your mind.

And, if you find your reasoning mind hog-tied and shoved in the trunk?

Well, just know that you're in for a hell of a ride.

CHAPTER TWO

COMMON SENSE (AND THE LACK THEREOF)

MY FATHER-IN-LAW, Don, was a highly successful Realtor in Rhode Island, a brilliant human being who understood that genuine connection and relationships are at the heart of everything from business and management to family, friendships, and community cohesion. He became so successful because he befriended everyone he met. People knew him, trusted him, and recommended him. He built a strong team because people genuinely wanted to work for him and with him.

Don's charm and engagement wasn't a ploy; it was genuine care and mindful connection.

Prior to launching his real estate career in the 1980s, Don worked as a collections supervisor for Sears. His office boasted the highest rate of collections, the highest employee satisfaction, the highest customer satisfaction, and the lowest turnover in the region. However, Don's boss was not impressed with the success of his office; rather, he decided that Don must be doing something wrong to get those kinds of numbers.

Of course, Don understood that a happy employee is a productive employee, and so he made sure to strategize happiness in a way that was beneficial for all. His team was composed mostly of working mothers who often found themselves in the sick-child dilemma, and as such would call in sick because a child was ill and they needed to stay home. Of course, this meant that they'd miss their shift, collections would drop, and they would miss a day's pay. So, Don instituted a policy of "flex time" before flex time was even a thing. If these mothers could find someone to watch their child, they could come in and work their shift later that day, make their calls, and not lose pay. He also implemented split shifts to meet the scheduling needs of his employees while meeting the business needs of the office.

His boss, instead of rewarding Don's creativity—which had clearly led to increased productivity and revenue—doubled down on "the way things have always been done." Of course, collections went down and revenues immediately dropped—but still, the boss insisted on playing by the old rules.

"No common sense," Don would say. "They had no common sense at all."

The "common sense" to which Don referred was simply meeting people where they are, providing what they needed within reason, and building trusting relationships so everyone could perform well within their job function and feel valued and appreciated. So, he disobeyed his boss and continued to do things his way, maintaining strong relationships with his team and even with the customers from whom they were collecting, right up until he retired from Sears and launched his successful chapter in real estate.

You're probably thinking, "Yup, that boss had no common sense at all (SMH)." And you're not wrong. But take a moment to reflect on how often you, your bosses, and your team members follow policy even when it doesn't make sense. Far too many of us never question the rules that have been set for us. Following instructions doesn't make you a Bad Boss. But doing it blindly, especially when it's hurting your team? That's not common sense. That's mindlessness.

Now, let me be clear. I'm not dissing policies. Policies are created for good reasons, but certain situations—particularly those involving individual human beings—call for creativity and a departure from the norm. This is where mindfulness in your leadership approach can come in really handy.

But let's step back to why so many bosses—maybe even you—prioritize policy over common sense. And let's think about why we, as professionals of any ilk, accept this practice as normal and perpetuate it even when it creates conflict, anxiety, or goes directly against "common sense."

Well, in order to understand how we got here, we need to look at where we come from. So, let's talk about social and emotional conditioning. (Don't worry. You'll see where I'm going with this in a moment.)

THE GOOD, THE BAD, AND THE POLICY

There has always been a hierarchical structure to labor and work. In fact, the modern terms we use for workplace organizational structures are steeped in notions of power, control, indentured servitude, and even slavery.

The word "boss" originates from the Dutch word *baas*, which translates to "master." It was strategically adopted in American culture to demonstrate labor hierarchy while avoiding any associations with slavery, which was falling into disfavor in the dawning years of the Industrial Revolution (although it would be decades longer before it was made illegal). Similarly, the term "supervisor" originated from the Latin word *superverdere*, which translates to "overseer"—again, a word chosen in an attempt to distance work hierarchy from indentured servitude or slavery. The Latin term *labor* means to toil or exert oneself physically.

We have been conditioned over many generations to view labor as a hierarchical power structure in which power and money are the ultimate rewards—but also to believe that those things are limited and that not everyone can have them. So, who's worthy of this limited power? Generational belief systems say it's those who work hard and follow the rules.

Many of us are still operating according to that belief system. We think that if we play the game, climb the ladder, and above all, *follow the rules*, there will be a reward for us at the end of the journey. And, to some degree, this might be true. If we're "good" employees, we might get promoted. We might become managers, supervisors, and even executives, achieving more power, more pay, and the chance to be part of the rules-setting class. In most places, if we want to be a power holder, we must comply with and enforce the rules. Only after years or even decades of adherence will we actually be in a position to change the rules we don't like—but by then, we're conditioned to think, "I got here by following these rules, so everyone else should do the same."

In fact, unless your work culture is highly mindful, emotionally intelligent, and people-centric, I can pretty much guarantee that the "game" is rigged to reflect the direct experience of the C-suite, executive leadership team, or board of directors.

They're making the rules based on what worked for them. But what worked for them might not—in fact, probably won't—work for most people in the organization. And, if there's a lack of mindfulness at the rule-making level, the things that don't work are unlikely to change.

No common sense there, my friend, but it happens all the time. It's classic social and emotional conditioning, and it plays into every aspect of work culture and leadership.

For example, one of my clients, whom I'll call Jeff, struggled immensely when the COVID-19 pandemic hit, and his entire team was forced to work remotely. The pre-pandemic policy was an on-site eight-to-five workday with a one-hour lunch break. Meetings were held in one of three conference rooms, and remote work was discouraged except under very special and specific circumstances.

Well, COVID-19 was definitely a "special circumstance."

Jeff, as president of the organization, was distraught. He feared that work wouldn't get done and that his people would drop *all* the proverbial balls. So, he immediately instated a new company-wide policy. Everyone had to log on to Zoom at 8:00 a.m., remain on camera all day, and log off at 5:00 p.m.

"That way," he explained, "we won't feel isolated. It will be just like being in the office."

Unsurprisingly, his new policy was met with a resounding "Are you freaking serious, Jeff?"

Most people balked. Many chose non-compliance. When Jeff threatened punitive action against those he perceived as insubordinate, the employees, all fifty-six of them, obediently turned on their cameras at 8:00 a.m. the following Monday, and total chaos unfolded.

Talk about malicious compliance.

Jeff, a happily divorced single dude living in a sweet artist's loft in the city, was not prepared for the cacophonous onslaught of his employees' realities: couples working at opposite ends of the kitchen table, babies crying, suddenly-homeschooled children interrupting their parents every few minutes to ask, "Mommy, what is the 'order of operations'?" "Why does Shakespeare talk so funny?" and the best, "Was the Diet of Worms, like, a nutrition plan or something?"

Adding to the chaos were dozens of barking dogs, cats perched on keyboards, and one very naughty ferret who kept stealing an employee's webcam.

On Tuesday, Jeff amended the policy. Animals and children should not be in the same space as employees during work hours. Period.

It was then that Paula, Jeff's executive assistant, called me in a panic. "Emily, there's going to be a mutiny if someone doesn't talk some sense into Jeff. Two people already quit after yesterday!"

I called Jeff immediately. "Dude, what's happening over there?"

As it turned out, Jeff was suffering from what I like to call "policy powerplay." He was totally overwhelmed and struggling to handle the uncertainty of the pandemic situation, so instead of collaborating with his team to determine the appropriate solution to this challenge, his response was to attempt total control. The stress of the situation turned on his amygdala "dimmer switch" and he was moving from a very emotional space.

"Have you asked your employees what they need in terms of support and how they would be able to work best until we 'flatten the curve'?" ("Flatten the curve." Remember that one? Ha!)

"I can't do that."

"Why not?"

"Because, as President, I have to make the decisions."

"Right. So … how's that working for you so far?"

Jeff put his head in his hands. "This whole situation is a mess. If you have a better idea, I'm all ears."

"Umm … maybe ask your employees what they need in terms of support and how they would be able to work best?"

"I can't do that …"

And round and round we went.

Finally, he agreed to let me facilitate a strategy session with the staff to determine what would work for everyone, since Jeff's policy clearly wasn't it.

Unfortunately, even though many employees suggested valid and workable solutions, Jeff struggled with the flexibility required to handle the various needs that were voiced. It was "too ambiguous," he declared, and instead implemented a whole new set of policies, many of which contradicted one another and all of which caused additional anxiety and frustration for the already overtaxed team. Within six weeks, the employee rolls dwindled to a mere thirty-eight people.

In late 2021, I facilitated a Mindful Leader Practice™ workshop for a company at which Jeff was a new employee. Though he didn't provide specifics, he told me that he'd been let go by his board of directors three months into lockdowns.

Apparently," he said, a bit sheepishly, "I didn't handle the pandemic transition well."

I didn't say, "No shit, Sherlock." At least, not out loud. (Look at me mastering my emotional brain!) Besides, I was genuinely sorry that he was forced to abandon ship on the company he had built from the ground up. That must have totally sucked.

After a pause, Jeff asked, "Will you be teaching us any strategies for navigating uncertainty in this course?"

"Absolutely," I promised.

Don't worry, I'll be teaching them to you, too.

Hierarchy, power, and control are delicate concepts. Wielding them well requires thought, strategy, and vision. It also requires intense self-awareness, empathy, and humility—all of which can be far more easily accessed when we are practicing mindfulness.

To become a mindful leader, you must drop the belief that power is finite or limited to a certain group. Thinking this way generates a lack mentality from which fear and incivility can arise. If power and influence are finite, someone can take them away. If opportunities are finite, we can be shut out or denied our chance. This dynamic creates competition, jealousy, conflict, paranoia—and, in extreme cases, flying cell phones and keys. All of the above are ingredients of a toxic work culture. All can be minimized or even eradicated when leaders practice mindfulness.

Great leaders know that power is granted, not taken. That it is fluid and dynamic, not static. They are comfortable with their limitations. And, most of all, they share power as a strategy for professional development, team cohesion, and employee retention. As Jeff learned, no one wants to feel like they don't have a choice, or that they are prisoners to policy. Letting go of the reins is sometimes the best way to stay on the horse.

So, how do you define power in your leadership experience?

What does "having power" mean to you? And how do you think power and policy are related? Download some helpful journal prompts at **unfunkyourselfbook.com**.

YOU CAN'T MANAGE YOUR WAY INTO GOOD LEADERSHIP

In addition to policy power, leaders also wield emotional power. We have the power to create conflict or dissolve it. We have the power to lift people up or break them down. And as long as we're walking around in a state of unawareness, we may be clueless as to whether we are doing any, or all, of the above.

Yes, we're back here again, talking about emotions. But when you think about it, as leaders, we don't really manage businesses. We manage tasks that are carried out by the humans we lead. And humans, as we know, are emotional first and logical … sometimes.

We humans are incredibly creative, industrious, and brilliant, and also insecure, judgmental, fearful, and messy as hell, thanks to our propensity to react from that emotional brain. And, since most of us aren't even aware that our dimmer switch is on and we're operating from our emotional brains, it can feel impossible to do anything differently, even when we gain some awareness of how our reactivity is undermining our relationships and results.

Now, if we're not practicing mindfulness, and at least attempting to remain in control of our own emotional brain, how can we effectively lead *other people* who are also stuck in their emotional brains?

The simple answer is, we can't.

This is why many bosses manage instead of lead. Management is task-based and looks at objectives, goals, and trajectories. We don't have to understand people's messiness in order to clearly state that Policy X plus Action Y will create Outcome Z.

But leadership is about engagement, connection, inspiration, and guidance. While managers focus on compliance, leaders enroll people into a greater vision that makes everyone want to do better. Leadership is social and emotional, and must be addressed before any managerial tasks can be successful.

We aren't meant to manage human beings. We manage things like schedules, tasks, and ordering the best snacks for the team meeting. Humans are meant to be inspired, led, and guided so they can bring their talents to bear as they manage tasks to meet the business's goals. If leadership is funked up, all the KPIs in the world won't make a difference to productivity, engagement, or any other human factors.

Again, if you've been managing instead of leading, it's not your fault. After all, when leaders are promoted, they're often thrown into "management" classes, given "management" guidelines, and even called "managers." Even the pathways to management are devoid of opportunities to learn real leadership skills.

No wonder we're all confused.

Here are some common ways that people find themselves in leadership roles. Maybe one or more of them apply to you.

- *Being Good at The Thing.* Many times, managers are promoted into their positions because of skills and talents they demonstrated at the job they were doing as an individual contributor. Some folks invest in and receive extra training so they can be really good at the job they're doing. Their talents and skills were noticed, and they were offered an opportunity to manage a team of people doing The Thing. Now, we have a manager who's highly skilled at doing The Thing, but essentially unprepared to lead staff. They soon realize that their ability to do The Thing doesn't translate at all into doing the thing they're doing now, which is leading a team. In such situations, people either revert to micromanaging so they can still do The Thing and continue to prove their value, or they become too permissive and people-pleasing because that worked well for them as an individual contributor.

- *Paying Your Dues.* Some managers get promoted into their positions because of seniority. Institutional knowledge and loyalty to the company is important and helpful, but it doesn't create good leaders on its own. Often, promotions of this nature create strife because now the promoted person is managing people who were once their lateral peers. The boundaries of boss/colleague/friend become blurry, and judgment about the new boss's worth and deservingness can run rampant.

- *Having Great Chops.* Some managers are hired because they have an excellent resume overflowing with the technical skills necessary to meet the logistical needs of the role. But sometimes, they aren't vetted for culture fit and leadership skills. Often, when a new leader arrives on scene, they'll feel the need to "prove themselves," so they make changes immediately, causing the existing staff to freak out and diminishing trust from the outset.
- *Knowing the Big Boss.* We're seeing lots of chatter about "nepo babies" in Hollywood right now, but nepotism is and has always been rampant in the business world. Family-owned businesses in particular are often built with legacy in mind, passing the torch from one generation to the next. However, even in publicly traded companies, many bosses prioritize bringing in friends with knowledge. I can't tell you how many times I've met a new executive or upper-management hire who got a foot in the door not because of their skills, but because their dad played golf with the CEO, they went to college with the daughter of the department head, or they had some other family or network connection. Having an "in" is great, but it doesn't guarantee leadership skills. In fact, in my experience, people hired this way are often among the least equipped to lead, because their "nepo baby" status leads them to feel overly

> secure in their positions. When you basically can't be fired, why change or develop your skills?

All of these pathways are feasible and common ways to become a boss, and they are all missing the same thing: leadership training. When we were getting great at The Thing, putting in the time, writing our kick-ass resume, or networking with those family connections, we weren't thinking at all about how we would manage our anxiety or anger the first time we had to say to an employee, "I need to see you in my office."

SELF-AWARENESS IS THE FIRST STEP TO UN-FUNKED LEADERSHIP

Whether you're leading a huge team of people or leading yourself to do the best job you can do, the skill set that will serve you best in any and all professional situations is self-awareness.

Self-awareness—being aware of, present to, and non-judgmental of who you are, how you feel, and why you think and behave as you do—is a direct byproduct of mindfulness. It's also a precursor to skillful communication, which we'll be exploring later in this book.

Being willing to look at yourself objectively requires both courage and a gigantic dose of humor. It also requires openness and humility, and the willingness to surrender to the fact that you are a flawed and beautiful product of your own experience.

While you're reading this book, there will be times when you want to toss it across the room and tell me to "funk" right off. Go ahead. I don't mind. What you're about to dive into is hard work. Mindfulness isn't smooth and pretty. It's not an intellectual dive into theoretical ideas and lofty ideals. It is a challenging trek through the reeking swamp of your own flaws, missteps, and failures. There's lots of stuff hiding under the surface that you won't want to see, let alone touch.

Sounds fun, right?

Well, maybe not fun. I can't promise you fun. But I can promise that, if you approach this process of un-funking yourself through mindfulness wholeheartedly, it will be cathartic, incredibly freeing, and the best damn thing you will ever do for your professional career.

I'll be honest, there are hundreds of great leadership books out there, and a good portion of them are devoted to mindful leadership. (I should know. I have a somewhat unhealthy obsession—I mean, practice—of reading every leadership and business book I can get my hands on. And let's not mention the TED talk binges.) But this book is different. Not because it's "better," but because it was born out of raw, real experience. I mean, we're only in Chapter Two and I've already shared some of the most cringe-worthy moments of my professional life to date! Like you, I struggled to wrap my mind around my own funked-up leadership. I struggled to employ mindfulness and self-examination to compassionately accept my shortcomings and do better every time I screwed up. What you're getting in these pages isn't some "visionary theory" of great leadership. It's a roadmap to real, lasting change for both you and those you have the opportunity to lead, today and in the future.

In the coming chapters, we will excavate the three pillars of Mindful Leadership—holistic communication, emotional intelligence, and self-compassion—and create a customized practice of mindfulness that you can lean into no matter how swampy your emotional mind currently is.

As you follow along and put into practice the various mindful shifts, you will see immediate results at work, at home, and in your community. You will accomplish more and worry less. Your patience and inner calm will increase while your stress levels decrease. Your capacity for empathy will improve as your perspective about your colleagues and reports expands. And, paradoxically, your leadership approach will become more strategic and streamlined as your leadership methods and behaviors become more thoughtful.

So, my friend, let's get un-funky!

CHAPTER THREE

WHAT'S IN YOUR ATTIC?

DARLA, A DRIVEN YOUNG PROFESSIONAL in a competitive role, was one of my most challenging coaching clients, like, *ever*. She took her job very seriously, and any criticism of her work, or even of the department she led, was received like a personal attack.

Per her request, our first coaching session took place at a coffee shop. She was a regular there, and as soon as she walked in the barista knew exactly what to make: a double espresso with six sugars.

"It's how I keep going in the afternoon," she declared as she gulped down the brown sludge in her cup. "Don't want the post-lunch slump!"

We sat down, and without prelude, she dove right in. "My boss hired you because he wants me to be a 'leaner' leader. I want to squeeze every ounce of productivity possible from myself and my team. We have to be the best."

She leaned in, her face intent. "I'm not interested in coming in second. I have *always* been the best."

I wasn't sure if that was a promise or a threat. "Well, I'm not really a lean coach," I said. "I focus on improving team cohesion and communication. So, it's possible that I'm not a good fit."

"I appreciate your candor, but I'll be the judge of that. We'll give you a try and see how this goes."

Okay, then.

As the conversation unfolded, I discovered that Darla had been a star athlete throughout high school, receiving a full-ride athletic scholarship to college. Frustrated by academic life, she opted to leave and pursue work instead. She didn't realize at the time that her struggles in class were due to undiagnosed dyslexia and ADHD.

Darla held herself to a very high standard. An almost unattainable standard, in fact. She constantly compared herself to other people and became jealous if someone achieved something ahead of her, or that she didn't think was possible for her. She mentioned a long-standing rivalry between her and a woman named Mina, her counterpart in another department. Honestly, I wasn't sure her counterpart even knew they were competing, but Darla made sure she tracked every move her nemesis made—her meetings, her department's productivity levels, her turnover rates, even when she left work early or took a lunch longer than sixty minutes. The amount of intel she rattled off was staggering, as I'm sure the look on my face indicated.

"I'm not obsessed, I'm invested," she said, smiling.

I asked my standard discovery questions to get an idea about her stance on leadership.

"What is your goal for our coaching?"

"To become and stay the best division in our department."

"How would your colleagues describe you?"

"They'd say I get shit done."

"What are the strengths of your team?"

"They're tough. They're hard workers."

"How do you celebrate success?"

"Success means we're doing our jobs. I don't give out medals for people doing their jobs."

"How do you bounce back from failures?

"Failure is not an option. *I* don't fail—but if someone on the team does, I fix it ASAP."

I asked her what she did in her free time, and she mentioned about six different hobbies, including being part of two community soccer leagues.

"What do you do to relax?"

"Relaxing's not my thing," she said. "If I'm not busy, I feel lazy."

Oh, boy, did I have my work cut out for me. There was something much deeper than just superhuman motivation going on here.

We had a few more sessions, during which we dug a bit deeper into the "why" behind Darla's productivity push, but I felt like I was hitting a brick wall with her.

Then, one day, I received a call from Jed, Darla's boss. He was completely distraught.

"Darla's in the hospital," he told me in a panicked voice. Apparently, she'd been at her desk when she started struggling to breathe. She brushed it off, but then started vomiting and hallucinating. Something was really wrong. Someone on the team called 9-1-1, and she was taken to the ER in an ambulance.

When I was able to see her, the first thing she said was, "Oh, that was so embarrassing. I really messed up, didn't I? What did Jed say to you?"

Her first concern wasn't for her health and the various

factors that led to her having a heart attack at her desk, but that she would be perceived as having failed in some way.

"I'll bet Mina is scheming for my job already."

"How are you feeling physically?" I asked her.

"Fine," she said. "Totally fine. I just want to go home and get back to work. I bet it was all the coffee. So, no more coffee. I'll just switch to green tea."

I wasn't going to let her off the hook that easily. "What else are you going to do? Like, to reduce your stress levels and get some rest so your body can heal?"

Darla's face crumpled. "I'm afraid to think about it," she admitted. "I'm not sure I know how to change. Where would I even start? And I can't not go to work, Emily! Jed will find someone to replace me."

Darla existed in shifting pools of fear, one spilling into the next. Everything was a threat or a challenge—including, now, her own body. She was reactive as a rule, and totally out of touch with both herself and those around her. I'd heard the genuine care and worry in Jed's voice when he called me. He wasn't going to let her go that easily.

I worked with Darla for six months. We did not, in fact, squeeze every drop of productivity from everyone on her team. Nor did we increase her personal output. But we did begin the process of introducing mindfulness to her daily life, both personally and professionally.

The truth was, Darla didn't have an identity separate from work. She had an intense fear of failure and therefore needed lots of external validation. In her mind, she'd failed as an athlete—"the one thing I was good at," she told me—and believed that she'd disappointed her parents. She was constantly concerned about what her parents and siblings thought of her, and when she joined the workforce, that concern extended to anyone in a position of authority. Mina, her "competition" in the other department, was in the role of sibling in Darla's work family, and the rivalry was just as intense.

She judged herself harshly, and came to realize that she did this so that when someone else judged her, she'd know that she'd beaten them to it, and that they couldn't say anything worse about her than she'd already thought about herself. No one could ambush her, and no one could surprise her. She wore her self-criticism like armor.

"What if who you are could just be enough?" I asked her one day.

"What does that even mean, Emily?" she replied. "If I'm 'enough,' how will I get better? And what the hell does me thinking I'm enough have to do with my and my team's performance?"

"You've got to know who you are and what stuff matters to you before you can know who anyone else is. And you have to know people before you can lead them. If you don't learn to do this, you'll always see yourself and others through a lens of comparison and assumption. And that means you won't see their gifts. You won't see how to motivate them, or support them, or help them grow. Or be more productive," I added, knowing only the last point would get her attention.

For a long time, I wasn't sure my coaching was helping. But toward the end of our time together, Darla made some major breakthroughs. She finally gave herself permission to lean into her authenticity, recognize her truths, and acknowledge the untruths she'd been living.

As it turned out, Darla didn't actually like soccer. But her mom was a soccer star, as was her older sister, so she played to make them proud. She never wanted to go to college at all, but no one else in her family had strayed from the four-year degree path, so she didn't think she could, either. So many of her decisions came from a place of measuring up. But now that she understood the reasoning behind them, she could let them go. The first thing she did was ditch the soccer league; instead, she took up painting and Pilates, which she truly enjoyed.

And the rivalry with Mina? Well, Mina reminded Darla a lot of her older sister. Mina had skills and talents that Darla felt she lacked. She perceived Mina as being more attractive and likable than her. But once she viewed her feelings through a more mindful lens, she realized that she *liked* Mina, and was actually scared that Mina didn't like her. Darla found the courage to invite Mina to lunch and suggested they connect and collaborate often to build cohesion between their teams. Mina accepted, and they are currently building a strong partnership in the company.

By the time our engagement was complete, Darla had completely adjusted her leadership style and was beginning to guide her team members in the ways that best suited their needs instead of putting all her energy into productivity. She's also embraced her neurodiversity instead of trying to hide it, and has even found some hidden skills that make her even more valuable to the company. Her team is still "winning"—in fact, they're even more successful than they were before—but they're no longer playing the same game. The new game is one of mindfulness, a consistent, flowing journey of learning and acceptance.

Today, Darla is still a go-getter. I doubt that will ever

change. But she's happier, healthier, more mindful, and has a better perspective on what "success" means to her and to everyone in her orbit.

UNPACKING YOUR MIND

As we covered in Chapter One, mindfulness is awareness that arises through paying attention, on purpose, in the present moment, non-judgmentally.

Mindfulness is a way of being, certainly. But to get to a place where it's natural enough to *become* a way of being, we need to approach it as a practicable skill, much like playing an instrument, painting, or making a really good cup of coffee. Just as with any other skill, if you want to get good at being mindful, you need to practice.

As I've shared, this book is rooted in not only my expertise as a coach but also in my personal experience—in particular, the hard, cringy, humiliating, and sometimes hilarious lessons that brought me to a different level of self-compassion, empathy, and ultimately sanity through mindfulness.

To communicate what I've learned about mindfulness and its application in leadership, I'll use a lot of (often bad) analogies, beginning with this one:

Your mind is like an attic. Or maybe a barn, or a cellar, or a cupboard under the stairs. And starting now, we're going to explore it with the intention of becoming more aware of what's actually motivating you, pushing you, pulling you, and influencing your decisions as a person and a leader.

Whatever household storage area to which you compare your mind, we can agree that there's a lot of stuff in there.

There's a bunch of clutter and cobwebs and dust. And probably some weird fingerprint portraits from first grade. (It's cool. We all drew purple blob people at some point.)

Some stuff in our minds needs to be accessed often. Like toilet paper, dry goods, and all the good cookies you're hiding from your kids because they and their greedy little friends will eat them all if you don't. (Parent tip: if you don't have an attic or cellar in which to hide cookie contraband, stick them in a Raisin Bran box in the pantry. Kids will *never* look there.) This level of mind-stuff is what you need for daily functioning: quick recall, your daily routines, how to drive your car, the meetings on your calendar, whose birthday is coming up, the running mental grocery list … you get the picture.

Then, there are things we only need to access once in a while, like the good dishes, holiday decorations, and that one tacky vase from Aunt Tammy that you *must* display on the mantle when she comes to visit so she doesn't have a cow. This is stuff you don't always think about but can bring forth when necessary: sixth grade math, Grandma's carrot cake recipe (or, at least, where you put the recipe card), random song lyrics, and John Hughes movie lines. (Okay, that last one might just be me. And basically every Gen-Xer I know.)

Then, there's the stuff way in the back. Boxes that haven't been opened in years. High school yearbooks, college textbooks, photo albums handed down through generations. Moth-eaten linens. Dusty side tables with crooked legs. Artwork that your parents saved for God knows what reason, but now you can't throw it away because *nostalgia*. This stuff is fuzzy around the edges and yellowed with time, but given the right stimuli—scents, sounds, the sight of the sun streaming through the clouds just right—it will all come rushing back.

Then, there's the dark stuff. The boxes we shove under the eaves and in the dark corners. Boxes filled with toxic, sharp, painful, scary stuff. We don't mean to collect this stuff, but it ends up in our head space anyway, and even though we do our best to avoid it, we can feel it there, lurking like Pennywise in the sewer. These are our agonizing memories of humiliation, rejection, regret, loss, grief, heartbreak, unresolved pain, and shame. Some of these boxes contain stuff that never even happened, but we loaded them with what-ifs and ought-tos and maybes, and then used them to prop up a whole pile of assumptions. These memories probably escape from time to time even though you've tried to staple these boxes shut. And if your storeroom gets flooded by a big, emotional event (or your attic roof falls in under too much pressure), watch out: the contents of those boxes will seep out and make a giant mess.

Why does all of this matter to leadership? Well, everything in our attics, basements, cupboards, and crannies—all of those memories and experiences and our habitual responses to them—affect how we function on a daily basis. We have patterned our current worldview, even our whole personality, on experiences from our distant and recent past. We build our beliefs around those experiences, and we structure our behaviors and reactions around those beliefs. The scaffolding of our existence is anchored by the boxes in our attic, and they affect *everything*—including how we show up at work and how we lead.

Just look how the resentment, fear, judgment, and jealousy in Darla's boxes created her entire work experience. Her experience of needing to compete with her sister, live up to her mom's achievements, and always exceed expectations informed not only how she showed up at work, but also pushed her to make work, and specially her results at work, the focus of her entire existence. It also influenced how she saw her employees and peers, particularly Mina, and created a barrier to partnership and understanding that was completely one-sided and ultimately impacted her well-being.

That second part—how she saw her employees and peers—is really important to the leadership discussion. How she saw her team became how she led her team. And until we began working together, she saw her team mostly as tools for "winning" a game no one else knew they were playing.

Here's another example. Imagine if, as a leader, you held an unconscious bias against working moms. Maybe your mom worked long hours and wasn't there for you, and you saw her as being unreliable, or maybe your first boss was a mom and, as an individual, didn't do a good job of balancing her work and home life. So, when one of the moms on your team puts her hat in the ring for a big project, you may (again, unconsciously) pass her over for the project because you think she isn't reliable enough to handle it, even though she's the most qualified candidate and you have absolutely no evidence that she is unreliable as an individual. Maybe you think, "This will be a lot to take on, and she's got a family to tend to, so she won't be able to give it 100 percent," and never even offer her the opportunity to evaluate the pros and cons for herself.

This is super funked-up boss thinking. Just because (in this theoretical example) there's a box in a dark corner of your attic labeled "unreliable moms" leaking fumes into your space, you end up making a biased and flawed decision and maybe even limiting the career of someone who could be a top performer.

Strong leaders take the time to clean out their attics regularly and take an inventory of what's in there, even if they're not quite ready to get rid of it yet. Bad Bosses keep chucking stuff in there until something explodes, crashes through the floor, or the cops show up with a search warrant.

If you haven't already guessed, mindfulness is how we unpack the boxes in your attic. And when we do that unpacking without judgment and without all the should've-would've-could've—what Gary Gulman refers to as the "holy trinity of regret"—we learn a lot about our behaviors and motivations, and about how we can more comfortably and intentionally exist within our reality.

Leading mindfully requires at least some level of behavior change, and behavior change requires a heap of self-awareness. Self-awareness—the real kind, the kind that's messy and challenging and oh-so-fucking-worth-it—requires mindfulness. You need to get up into that inner attic and get down and dirty with what you find there. You cannot fine tune your skills (behavior) if you do not first understand the roots of the behavior that requires tuning.

Your journey into mindfulness and self-discovery will look different than it does for anyone else, because all of our boxes contain different stuff, but the process is fairly universal—and the process is *practice*.

This is where the work begins.

You can read this book cover to cover, laugh at my jokes, and nod your head at shared experiences, but until you dive in and do the work, that fine tuning won't happen. I like to joke that I have a magical personality (my jokes make people disappear!) but this book isn't a magical antidote to your funked-up boss behavior. The work you put in, and the info you're learning, *is*.

THE PILLARS OF MINDFULNESS

From here on, every chapter in this book will include at least some element of reframing and shifting your mindset toward mindfulness to further your understanding of yourself and your leadership. There will be plenty of opportunities throughout the rest of the book to stop and reflect, to journal, and/or to meditate on the topic. Leaning on my training as a certified meditation practitioner and teacher, I've developed helpful tools for you to start or expand your mindfulness practice specifically through the lens of being a leader.

(Remember, you can find audio versions of the guided breathing and visualization exercises as well as a guidebook/journal at **www.unfunkyourselfbook.com**.)

So, this is a great place to introduce a fundamental piece of the mindfulness puzzle—or, more accurately, nine fundamental pieces, these being the nine attitudes of mindfulness as introduced by Jon Kabat-Zinn.

These nine "attitudes" are:

- *Non-Judgment.* Mindfulness is cultivated by bearing impartial witness to your own experience, which can be challenging because we are constantly judging and reacting to inner and outer stimuli based on previous experiences. We come by this honestly, because it's part of our primal brain's protection behavior. The work is in learning to step back and observe the thoughts rather than react to the stimuli. When we pay attention to the activity of our own mind, we quickly discover that we are constantly producing judgments about our experience.

- *Patience.* Patience is wisdom in demonstrating that we know and accept that sometimes things must progress in their own time. Someone might want to help a chick hatch from its egg by breaking open the eggshell. The chick would not benefit from this. The chick can only hatch in its own time and the process cannot be rushed.
- *Beginner's Mind.* Many of us are know-it-alls and we miss the splendor of the present moment, so we often miss out on the splendor of life. Too often we allow our assumptions and beliefs about what we think we know to prevent us from seeing things as they really are. We take the ordinary for granted and fail to notice that everything, even the mundane, can be extraordinary. To appreciate the present moment, we need to cultivate a "beginner's mind," a mind that is willing to see everything as if for the first time.

- *Trust.* Developing a basic trust in yourself, your feelings, and your needs is an integral part of a mindfulness practice. Trusting your intuition and your own authority, even if you make some mistakes along the way, is far better than always seeking external validation and guidance. When something feels good or when something does not feel right to you, it's best to trust and honor those feelings.
- *Non-Striving.* Think about your daily life. It's full of to-do lists and we are constantly striving for a purpose, to get something done or go somewhere. But in the attitudes of mindfulness, striving can be counterproductive because meditation is different from all other human activities. Though it takes work and energy, meditation is actually non-doing. The only goal is for you to be yourself, which you already are, and be comfortable in that space.
- *Acceptance.* Acceptance means acknowledging things as they actually are in the present moment. If you have an injury, accept that you have an injury. If you are overweight, accept that as the description of your body at this moment. It doesn't mean that we can't change this reality, but we have to accept reality as it is. And not judge it. Acceptance is usually reached after we have gone through very emotion-filled periods of denial, sorrow, and anger.

- *Letting Go.* Non-attachment is fundamental to the practice of attitudes for mindfulness. When we start paying attention to our inner experience, we discover that there are certain thoughts and feelings and situations that our mind seems to want to hold on to even if they are no longer a reality. Maybe you have a closet full of clothes that used to fit and you're hanging on to them in case they fit again. Maybe you remain in a relationship that has gone sour because it used to be good and maybe it will be again. Detach from what was and acknowledge what is. Letting go lifts the weight of should've-would've-could've so that we can accept and experience reality.
- *Gratitude.* Our emotional selves and our physical selves do not exist separately; they are intimately interwoven. Without diving down this rabbit hole, suffice it to say that our thoughts can trigger physiological changes in our body which affect our emotional and physical health. When you increase positive thoughts, like gratitude, you increase your sense of well-being and, perhaps, physical health.
- *Generosity.* The mindful attitude of generosity is another quality which, like patience, letting go, non-judging, and trust, provide a solid foundation for mindfulness practice. Cultivate generosity as a vehicle for deep self-observation

as well as an exercise in giving. Start with yourself. Give yourself the gift of self-acceptance or true relaxation. Practice feeling that you're deserving of these gifts, that you're deserving of them without obligation. Practicing authentic generosity to yourself opens the path to practicing generosity with others.

UN-FUNK YOUR AWARENESS

Take a moment to think about your colleagues.

- Who is your favorite colleague to work with? Why do you like this person so much? What are the qualities you admire about them? Do you feel an affinity with or similarities to them—and if so, what are they?
- Now, think about someone at work that you don't like. Why do you feel this way about this person? Do you feel uncomfortable with them? Do you dislike them because you feel a sense of rejection, or are you comparing your skills or education against theirs? Do you feel that they are difficult to work with—and if so, why?
- Now, try to apply the Nine Pillars of Mindfulness to both situations. How does this process feel? Where do you feel stuck?

Congratulations! You've just begun a self-awareness journey!

Hang on to the answers you just discovered, because you will want to visit these questions again as you have more mindfulness tactics to practice. As you're about to learn, there are many reasons why you like the first person and dislike the second. As you move through the book, you'll explore the roots of those feelings, and maybe have some big "a-ha" moments.

Thanks for sticking around. Onward into the swamp!

CHAPTER FOUR

WHO DO YOU THINK YOU ARE, BOSS?

I MOVED A LOT as a kid (and as an adult, too), and travel often for work, so I have experienced varied American cities, regions, and cultures at different stages of my life. Over dinner one night, my friend Josh asked me if I identified more as a Midwesterner or a New Englander, since I spent large parts of my childhood in both places.

"Well, a bunch of my life to this point has also been lived in Tennessee, so add Southerner to that list," I reminded him.

I have one of those brains that picks up and emulates accents, so I can mimic the accent and its variants from every place I've lived. It's a fun party trick (the only one I have, really, except for being able to hang a spoon from my nose). Friends and colleagues over the years have noticed that I often switch in and out of accents when telling stories; I sound totally Rhode Island when frustrated, and even more Tennessee when sipping whiskey.

But, back to Josh's question.

I used to joke that I was born a redneck and raised a Yankee and now I'm all confused. But that isn't true. I'm not confused, at all. But neither could I answer the question of my identity in a black and white manner. Partly, this is because I have spent so much time and energy dissecting what "identity" means, but also because, just like you, I am an amalgam of all of the places I've lived, the people I've encountered, the experiences I've had, and the associations and assumptions I've made between and about them all. It's complicated.

So, I did what any good social psychologist does in a moment like that: I deflected, and asked, "Well, how do *you* identify?"

"As a Midwesterner. Obviously."

"But what does it mean to be 'a Midwesterner'?"

He got stuck for a minute, then said, "I guess it means All-American, athletic, suburban, Christian. Umm …" As he thought more about the complexity of the question, he shrugged. "I actually have no idea what a 'Midwesterner' identity is. But that's my opinion about what it means to be Midwestern. For me."

Unsurprisingly, in describing "Midwesterner," he'd just perfectly described himself.

If he'd been a coaching client, my next question might have been, "So, how many of those are just you being you, and how many did you become in order to be more 'Midwestern'?" But that was a bit too heavy for a hot-wings-and-football Sunday night dinner.

We all do this. We do it all the time. We make a solid statement about our identity, and then hold on to our specific interpretation of that identity with all our might. Our identity, whether chosen, conditioned, or imposed, creates the parameters for our existence and how we "should" be. When someone doesn't fit the mold of identity we've created, we question its validity. "She can't be Southern. She doesn't even have a cast iron skillet! Bless her heart."

This, my friend, are where biases are born.

You don't have to look far to find examples of this. Political associations, collegiate affiliations, and even sports team fandoms create rigid identity lines in which you either exist or don't. If you do exist there, others will hold you there in order to preserve their own identities. You either color inside the lines or you're no longer "one of us."

In this way, identity serves as a means of protection. No human likes ambiguity. We like knowing what we are and where we belong. We like answers, even if the evidence is weak. Identity provides the answers we crave.

Identity also provides safety in a group, which we crave. Humans are hardwired to connect because there is safety in numbers; it's tribe mentality. When we find others who share a similar identity to us, we feel safe, accepted, and included. This isn't necessarily a bad thing. Sports teams share an identity, professions share an identity, even the *Star Wars* fandom shares an identity.

Let's dive into the *Star Wars* thing for a bit.

Across the interwebs, folks within the *Star Wars* fandom find certainty and comfort in knowing that they're in company with other scruffy-looking nerf herders who get just as excited about Millennium Falcon models and spouting movie lines as they do. They're bonded by their love of the *Star Wars* universe. When they walk into a fan convention, they know no one will judge their passion as nerdy or childish.

However, within the community, under the surface of unity, there's an ongoing debate about the authenticity of the various subgroups of the fandom. Some maintain that only the original trilogy counts, where others argue that the prequels and sequels complete the story. Some argue about character motivations or the reasons for events in the storylines. The debates can and often do become incredibly heated. Very judgy. Not mindful.

If you're not a *Star Wars* mega-fan, you're probably thinking, "Who cares? It's just a stupid movie franchise." But this sort of "identity splintering" happens not just in fandoms, but in other, perhaps more important and certainly more influential places in society. Like religion. Or politics. Or ethnicity. Or nationalism.

Think about the number of factions in the Christian faith alone. I have a friend whose über-Catholic paternal grandparents almost didn't come to her parents' wedding because her mom was—*clutches pearls*—raised a Protestant. Think about the debates and bickering that go on within various denominations about everything from strictness of interpretation, ceremony practices, authority, and leadership, just to name a few. Instead of creating unity under one religious umbrella, identity divides the larger group into factions.

Why do we do this? Why do we turn everything into a club that others must join or be rejected from? Why do we judge and gatekeep others based on our identity?

Well, again, we like certainty. We also like power.

In a fandom or hobby club, this is generally benign. Being "certain" about a fictional universe is pretty harmless. But certainty rarely serves us in complex, real-life situations involving complex, real people with their own unique layers of identity and bias.

Problems with identity crop up when we begin to use identity as armor to defend our position or as justification for gatekeeping or excluding others. When we feel threatened or are asked to go against the norms of our identity group, we may fear exclusion from the group. As a result, we may vehemently defend the group we feel beholden to and also amass allies to support our viewpoint—even if our viewpoint is incomplete or blatantly incorrect (we'll look at that a bit later).

Deeply ingrained identities are often at odds with mindful reflection, as well as with curiosity and empathy. If we want to lead more mindfully, we need to learn to think beyond what things "should" be and start seeing them for what they are.

If we aren't mindful about how we identify, our identity carries with it an inherent bias about how others are supposed to identify and/or what their identities are supposed to look like. We then begin labeling people, ideas, environments, movements, etc. as wrong, bad, scary, or weird—in other words, things we consider ourselves *not* to be, and that these other people *must* be because they are not like us.

Us = good. Them = bad.

Now, I'm not saying that having an identity, or even a whole slew of them, is bad. Identity is deeply personal. It is everything we think we are. It gives us purpose and meaning. It provides comfort and belonging, and gives us parameters for our existence and a sense of commonality with others. But when our identity becomes the primary tool for our decision-making, we are misusing it. We take what should be a tool for connection and turn it into a weapon.

Mindfulness asks us to pause, appreciate our viewpoints, our identity, and the experiences that brought us to what we believe, and then practice beginner's mind, acceptance, and non-judging, asking, "What am I not considering?" and "Why am I so upset by this other person's/group's identity and beliefs? Why do I feel triggered and threatened by this?"

When we take this mindful step, we often realize that, despite our differences, we are much more similar than dissimilar. More, we realize that, despite our differences or similarities, other people's identities do not in any way diminish our own. Empathy grows from this point.

HOW DO YOU IDENTIFY?

What identities and aspects of your experience make you who you are?

Identity is a story we tell ourselves and believe it as truth. It is a paradigm of existence. It can evolve over time, but if we examine it at any one point in our life, it feels fixed. Definite. Which is part of what makes it so interesting.

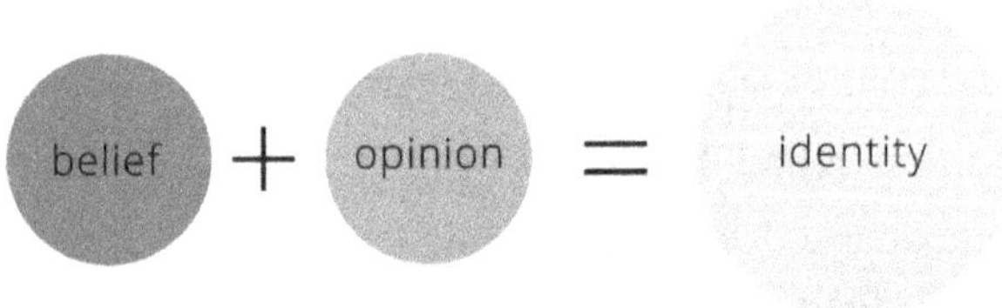

The beliefs and opinions that make up our identity come from many sources, some of which are interpreted differently per person. Beliefs and opinions stem from all sorts of areas including, but definitely not limited to, our base demographics: age, race/ethnicity, gender and gender expression. All of these are then affected by various influences like where and how we were brought up, what our education (formal and informal) was like, what our cultural and societal norms are, the social conditioning we experienced, and all of the random stuff that happened to, with, for, and around us. Big pieces of our identity might actually be the stories our parents told themselves, accepted as truth, and passed along to us. Many of those stories belonged to their parents, and theirs, and so on.

Some of those boxes in your attic contain generational stories that you've packed up and carried around with you even though they don't fit your truth and your life. In those boxes live nostalgia and inspiration, but in many cases, also guilt, shame, and comparison.

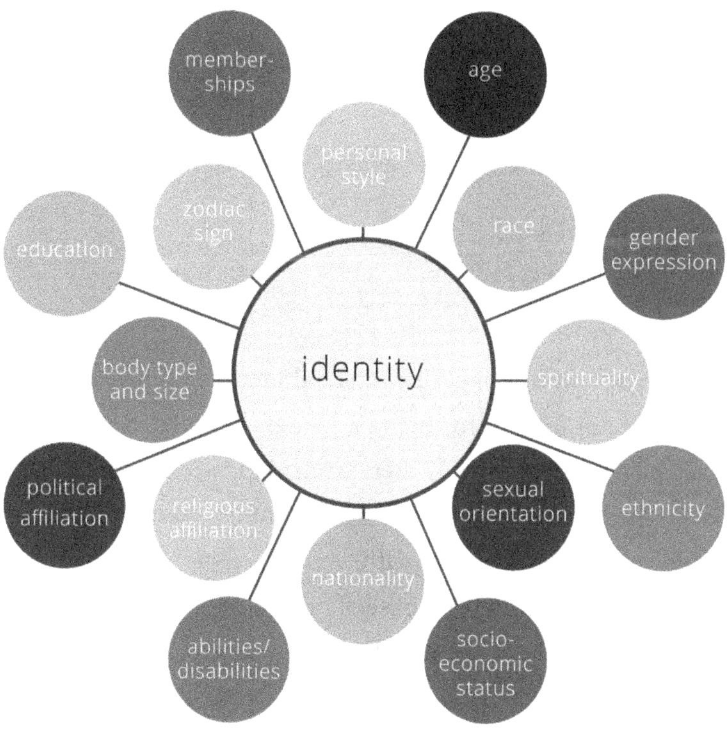

Those of us who have developed "rebel" identities have often done so as a way to push back against these established stories of who we are and what we should do. However, those stories remain a part of us as long as we're still operating from an "against" perspective and not letting go. If we let go of the stories, we'd have nothing to rebel against! There's identity in not identifying with our parents' identity. But holding on to their identity as a means to create our own is a mindless waste of energy.

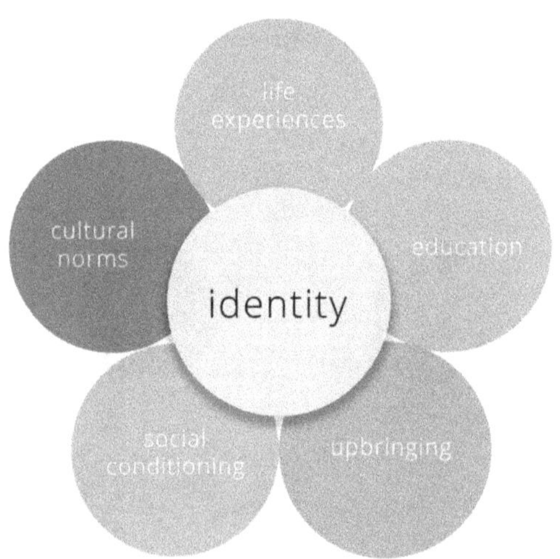

If you're wondering, my personal identity includes (but is definitely not limited to) being a white, cisgendered, mid-life, masters-educated, Gen-X metalhead. I'm also a wife, mom, sister, friend, Assertive/Inspiring communication style, intellectual, and animal lover with a neurospicy brain, a smart mouth, and a sophomoric sense of humor. I suppose I'm a bit of a rebel, especially in the starched-and-suited business spaces. I'm all about the combination of professional and comfortable with a splash of sass. How I present is important, but *what* I present is more so.

All of my identities mean different things to different people. For example, "Gen-Xer" to a Baby Boomer means "rebellious 80's kid," whereas to my Gen-Z kids it might mean "sort-of old person whose fashion sense is still stuck in the 90s." If someone were to ask my favorite bands, some would be like, "Rock on!" and others would say, "Oh, you're not a *real* metal-head because you don't like [insert random band here]." Back when I was a less mindful human, I might have engaged in a full-on argument about how my favorite bands set the whole damn tone, atmosphere, and *literal stage* for your shitty metal band, thank you very much. Today, I do less of that, because 1) your opinion is yours, and you're entitled to it, and 2) it doesn't matter all that much to me if you like my bands or not. We can both love our respective bands and happily bump around in the mosh pit of life.

Mindfulness is how we can respectfully disagree with our friends, spouses, families, coworkers, and yes, our employees, without needing to blow up the whole relationship. But to develop the mindfulness muscles to meet others where they're at, we need to understand *why* we feel so threatened when someone challenges our identity.

Remember the amygdala? Remember how it can't tell the difference between physical threat and emotional stress? Yeah, it's that. When our inherent need for connection with other humans runs headfirst into our inherent skepticism of other humans and our fear of the unknown, our brain flip-flops into a survival state and we become preemptively defensive, posturing for power and safety.

When someone disagrees with your opinion—especially if that opinion is inextricably tied to your identity—you will feel personally attacked. Your amygdala perceives this as danger and gets your system revved up for battle.

Yes, battle. Even if the disagreement is over something as silly as who the most influential metal band is.

The more central something is to our identity, the bigger the response when it's triggered. The metalhead argument might trigger some frustration and shouting. A hit to our religious, national, or political identity, however, might be enough to fracture a team, break up a family, or send a nation to war.

To make this all even more complicated, our brains *do not* like to be wrong. In fact, we hate being wrong so much that, when faced with factual evidence that contradicts our belief, we will defend our belief even more strongly than before. Welcome to cognitive dissonance.

According to Verywell Mind, cognitive dissonance is "the mental discomfort that results from holding two conflicting beliefs, values, or attitudes."(1) People seek consistency in their attitudes and perceptions, so any conflict between what we "know" and what is presented to us causes unpleasant feelings of unease or discomfort. Inconsistencies between what we believe and how we behave motivate us to engage in actions that will help minimize our feelings of discomfort, such as by rejecting or attacking the information (or the person presenting it), explaining away the evidence, or avoiding new information altogether.

---

(1) Kendra Cherry, MSEd. "Cognitive Dissonance and the Discomfort of Holding Conflicting Beliefs." *Verywell Mind*, Nov 2022. https://www.verywellmind.com/what-is-cognitive-dissonance-2795012

There are many examples I could cite here to show how cognitive dissonance works, but I'll stick with our (relatively) innocuous music theme.

My friend Deva is a punk-rock fiend. She's got all the markings (literal and figurative) of punk culture, including having the word "punk" tattooed on her left-hand knuckles. During a pre-mindful-Emily-era conversation about goodness knows what, she mentioned that the lead singer of Public Image Ltd. sounded a whole lot like the singer of Sex Pistols. And I said, "Well yeah, because they're the same person."

"Uh, no," she scoffed. "Sid Vicious is dead, so that's not possible."

I stared at her in disbelief. "Deva, Sid Vicious didn't sing, Johnny Rotten did. And now he's the lead singer for PIL."

Immediately, she got angry and told me I didn't know what I was talking about. So, I did what every good Gen-Xer would do: I Googled it. As the info on my phone was proving that I was, in fact, correct (which felt really good, because my own identity as a punk junkie was now being affirmed), I climbed even higher on my high horse and said, in a totally careless and not-at-all-mindful way, "How the hell can you call yourself punk if you don't even know who sang for the Sex Pistols?"

F-bombs flew. She cursed me up one side and down the other as she defended her position as a genuine punk. In her estimation, I had attacked her core identity as a punk rocker, and I was going to *pay*. More, she insisted that she was right about Sid Vicious being a singer. In her reactivity over my slight to her identity, she doubled down on her belief—even though she was literally holding the evidence in her hand, since she still hadn't given back my phone.

We eventually calmed down and talked about it, but our friendship hasn't been the same since. If I had known then what I know now, I would have handled that conversation totally differently.

Here's how something like this could play out in a professional setting.

I recently assisted a company with analyzing and updating their employee handbook. The executives were inspired to create a more inclusive workplace. I had to snicker a bit when I saw the policy that declared, "Visible tattoos, facial piercings, or multiple ear piercings are prohibited."

Oh, the irony that they'd hire *me*, with my visible arm tats, nose ring, and three holes in each ear—never mind my hair, which was definitely not a natural color at the time.

But really, good luck hiring anyone younger than a Baby Boomer with that policy. For many of us Gen-Xers, Millennials, and Gen-Zers, skin is a canvas onto which we can etch gorgeous and intricate stories of our existence, as well as the occasional Disney character or index finger mustache.

As we moved further into the "maintaining a professional appearance" portion of the handbook, there was a passage declaring that headwear of any kind was also prohibited and that facial hair needed to be "neatly groomed" at all times.

"What does 'neatly groomed' mean?" I asked. "And what provisions are you making for natural ethnic hair, protective styles, or religious and cultural requirements like hijabs?"

This room full of leaders—five older white men and one younger white woman—obviously hadn't considered this.

One of the men said, "Well, we don't really have those issues here."

"Well, if you're actively seeking diversity and value inclusion, you *should* have those issues here," I retorted.

I had to wonder how many Muslims, Sikhs, and folks of color hadn't been hired because they preemptively violated "grooming" policies based entirely on white identities and cultural expectations.

At another company, a client was prepping to hire twenty seasonal fundraising specialists, and I was helping vet the candidates. We conducted the phone screening together, determining who would progress to the in-person interview stage. As we moved from call to call, she would put the resumes in one of two piles, "yes" or "no."

As we ended a call with someone I thought was excellent, she scooted the resume into the "no" pile.

"Wait, why not this person?" I asked.

"Her accent was too heavy. I could barely understand her. She won't be good on the phones calling donors," she said.

"I could understand her just fine," I replied. "Plus, she'll be an excellent resource for calling Spanish- and Portuguese-speaking homes and businesses." The candidate, according to her resume, was trilingual in Spanish, Portuguese, and English.

"I don't know … I've had bad experiences with people like her."

"People like her? How do you mean that? Highly educated and experienced? Multilingual? Or do you mean heavily accented?"

That gave her pause as she was tiptoeing into some seriously dangerous waters.

Before we could move on to vetting the other candidates, we unpacked her identity story. I discovered that she'd had a bad experience with a coworker who happened to be Latina, and had applied that experience to all women of Latin American origin. As a result, she was willing to look past the vast qualifications of this particular candidate because of her personal beliefs related to Latina identity.

Not only is that type of thinking discrimination lawsuit territory, it's also hideously mindless, ignorant, and detrimental to the success of the entire organization.

After we identified the root cause of my client's bias, the candidate's resume was scooted into the "yes" category, and she was subsequently hired for the seasonal role. From what I understand, she was quite successful in her fundraising abilities, exceeding her financial goal as well as the goal for new sponsors—most of whom were Spanish- and Portuguese-speaking businesses.

UN-FUNK YOUR IDENTITY

- As a leader, how do you identify?
- What's your hierarchical view related to the folks you employ?
- On what norms do you base your hiring practice and employee handbook?
- Can you remember a time when you passed over a person or people for employment, promotion, or other considerations based on your identity paradigm and the expectations

that arise from it? (Be prepared for some cognitive dissonance on this one!)

- Now, think about the people you identified in the previous chapter. Is there anything about your identity, or theirs, that is contributing to why you do or do not like them?

Once you've answered the above questions, take a moment to honestly reflect on your leadership journey, what your expectations are, and how you're manifesting them in your identity paradigm. You can also download additional journaling prompts at **www.unfunkyourselfbook.com**.

Now that you are more mindful of what's happening in your decision-making, what will you do differently?

CHAPTER FIVE

THE NOTORIOUS ASJs

WHEN I WAS TWENTY-EIGHT, I was hired to implement a revenue-generating and employment training program for a transitional housing organization. My job was to get this project up and running and in the black as quickly as possible. The funding requirements were strict, and the window was short.

Due to the nature of the project and the requirements of its funding streams, most of my employees were single mothers who were participating in the housing program. It was from these women that I discovered my lack of empathy, although it took me a hot minute to understand it.

When I stepped into that role, I decided to hold all my employees to the same standards to which I held myself. They should demonstrate a strong work ethic, put in the effort necessary to learn and get the job done, and keep a positive attitude while doing it. I was determined to get these women in tip-top professional shape so they could remain in their new homes, reduce their dependency on programs, and be productive, happy people.

What I didn't understand at the time is that every single one of the values I held in such high esteem was relative. I had no idea what experiences these women had endured, or what unfathomable challenges they still faced. We had almost nothing in common in terms of what life had dealt us, and my lens of understanding was painfully narrow. My life experience wasn't peppered with trauma, fear, hunger, pain, and violence. My life experience, though challenging at times, was essentially one of safety. My basic needs were always met, and I had never been in a situation where I had to choose between my convictions and my survival.

My blindness was corrected in the most uncomfortable, challenging, and humbling ways.

Sofia was an energetic, hilarious employee who was always on time and always in a good mood. All of the employees and customers adored her. I decided that she was going to be my best success story out of this program.

When she called in sick one Monday, I didn't think much of it and told her I hoped she'd feel better soon. When she called in the next day, I was concerned, but, sadly, more about my staffing issues than her health. When she called in on Wednesday, I told her that I needed a medical note because this was just ridiculous. I was sure she was being lazy or just didn't want to come to work.

Later that day, Sofia came into my office. She didn't have a doctor's note. What she did have was two black eyes, one swollen almost shut, a broken front tooth, and multiple lacerations on the left side of her face. Her right-handed ex-boyfriend had found out where she was living and paid her a visit, assaulting her (again) as payback for leaving him. She came to say that she was sorry for disappointing me and to say goodbye.

That was the last time I saw Sofia; she and her three

daughters had to relocate, again, because her abuser had tracked her down, again, and he'd probably kill her next time.

When Shannon, who was always tired and seemed kind of flighty, didn't show up for work on Thursday, I began the write-up process for no-call-no-show. She was late a lot, but I cut her some slack because I knew she had a lot going on, and I was (I thought) a sympathetic boss. However, this time, something told me to hold off on the write-up. I was glad I did.

Shannon's social worker called me later that day to let me know that Shannon would be back to work toward the end of the week, but that she was currently in jail for prostitution.

"I'm sorry … what?" I asked.

Turns out, Shannon couldn't make ends meet working minimum wage alone. Her mother had died of an overdose when Shannon was fifteen, leaving her to fend for herself on the street. Hooking was a skill she'd learned so she could keep herself fed and clothed, and she still took some clients here and there when money was tight (hence her recent tiredness and spaciness). However, this time, a police officer who was one of her regulars decided to turn on her and arrested her—probably so he didn't have to pay up, the social worker observed acerbically—and now she was behind bars, waiting for a hearing, and in a financial hole due to the missed work hours. She'd have to go right back to the street if she wanted to make rent. It was, the social worker explained, a vicious cycle.

Vicious, I thought, *doesn't even* begin *to describe this.*

When I stepped into this job, my lens of understanding and identity—that of a white, middle-class, college-educated, cisgendered, physically healthy, emotionally stable, permanently housed woman—was not expansive enough to consider and empathize with the reality these women endured every day. I saw their plight, but it felt separate from my own existence. I was doing the noble work of "bettering" them, molding them into successful and productive employees, thinking that if they just "did it right" their problems would evaporate.

My eagerness to set them straight with traditional punitive measures was sorely misguided and completely out of touch with what my employees actually needed. If I truly wanted to guide them toward their personal versions of success, I would need to drop the high-and-mighty attitude and employ real empathy, understanding, compassion, and patience.

We approach our work, our relationships, and everything else in our lives through our own lens of understanding, which is shaped by our identity. Think of it as a sepia lens on a camera. We make assumptions based on what's been true for us, and when others don't live up to those assumptions, we judge, get offended, become guarded, or lose trust in them. We lean into stereotypes when we have little or no personal experience to give us certainty. We pass judgments based on what we would do or not do, or what others told us we should do or not do.

Through a sepia lens, the sky is gold. How dare someone say it's blue!

When we're being mindless, we don't even see that we *have* a lens. When we practice mindfulness, we can not only take off the lens but actually step out from behind the camera to see the whole picture. In releasing our need to have our viewpoint be the best and only one, we create massive opportunities for connection.

Now, let's be real: there is *nothing wrong* with your lens of understanding. Whether you grew up rich or poor, in the city or the country, with a loving family or without one, your lens is your perspective and your truth. But your truth doesn't apply as everyone else's truth. Understanding that everyone has their own lens of experience—and that this lens informs literally everything about them—is imperative to leading. You may never know the depth of others' truths, and, honestly, *their truths are not your business*. What you need to know is that these depths exist, and that, as a result, each person you lead requires a different approach.

There is absolutely no one-size-fits-all approach to communication. In fact, trying to "strategize" or systematize it would be totally funked up.

The best way to understand this is to go to pretty much any family reunion.

ASSUMPTIONS, STEREOTYPES, AND JUDGMENTS: THE FUNKED-UP COUSINS

In keeping with my promised bad analogies, may I introduce you to Identity's troublesome cousins: Assumptions, Stereotypes, and Judgment, aka the trifecta of mindlessness.

Most everyone I know has *those* cousins. You know, the ones who just can't keep themselves to themselves, and who like to stir up trouble at family reunions, weddings, and Uncle Doug's funeral. Well, A, S, and J are like that. They just don't know when to sit down and shut up.

Human beings don't like being uncomfortable, physically, emotionally, mentally, or otherwise. Maybe, like me, you snip the tags out of your concert tees because they're itchy reminders of the fact that you just spent $50 on a stupid tee shirt. Similarly, our brains dislike the discomfort of ambiguity, and so will itch and scratch and fidget until we either cut away or slap a label on the thing that's bugging us.

When something exists outside our norm, we aren't sure what to do with it, and we need answers *now* to inform our behavior. We make "educated guesses" that most often err on the side of the negative, because that's what we hear in the news or on socials or from Aunt Tammy, or because that's the only explanation available in our own limited worldview. *Oh, Shannon's late to work again. I guess she's too lazy to get up on time.* This is assumption.

Other times, we'll refer to some unsubstantiated story or comment we heard about The Thing We Don't Understand And Are Nervous About and run with it. Because we don't have any direct experience, a conflicting story, or mindful curiosity, we treat these stories as truth. *Well, Janine is a Millennial. You know how they are. Their iced mochaccinos and avocado toasts are* way *more important than getting to work on time.* This is stereotyping.

Still other times, we will determine that the thing we don't understand is bad or weird and, since we would never do, say, or be that thing, it must be *wrong, wrong, wrong*. This helps us feel better about ourselves and our own decisions, helps us justify our flaws because they're not as bad as someone else's, and even determine where we fit in on the "comparative suffering" scale. (More on that last bit later.) *The audacity to leave early to pick up her kids! I would never!* That's judgment.

Judgment is a real baddie because judgment leads to shame, and shame leads to suffering. When *Dune*'s Jessica Atreides taught Paul the axiom "fear is the mind-killer," she probably should have added, "and shame is the soul-killer." Shame is a nasty, debilitating monster that will devour whatever inner light and self-worth you have.

Then, there's cousin number four, Bad Info. This cousin is as awful as the rest, but sneakier. He's the one who hatches the plan, then stands on the sidelines snickering into his beer while those other dummies start the drama. We get Bad Info when Someone of Importance (a parent, a boss, a celebrity, a politician, a family member) states something as fact and it sticks in our brains, or when we file the results of our own assumptions and judgments away as truths. I mean, how many times have you read the liner notes only to find out that your favorite lyric was *not even close* to what the singer was actually saying? Maybe your cognitive dissonance even had you Googling it to be sure the liner notes weren't misprinted.

Now, song lyrics aren't (usually) central to our identities, but our beliefs are—and since our beliefs shape our actions, we need to examine them regularly for ASJ contamination.

Here's a perfect but innocuous example. I was always told that you have to wait thirty minutes after eating to swim. According to many staunch warnings from my mother, I'd get cramps if I used my arms and legs while my stomach was digesting food. At best, I'd be hurting. At worst, I could drown! However, according to the Mayo Clinic (which, no offense, Mom, bears more expert weight) this is total superstition. Go ahead and swim, kids.

To think, I wasted countless hours waiting for my food to digest and getting sunburns (which are *actually* dangerous) instead of cannonballing back into the cool water.

Yup, Bad Info is *definitely* an enabler.

Like Uncle Doug's moonshine, the ASJ cousins will give you a temporary high. They'll make you feel better in the moment. But, also like Uncle Doug's moonshine, when allowed to run rampant, those ASJs can turn you from a respected leader into the drunk cousin stumbling up the church aisle, tossing out insults, and horrifying the funeral-goers while Bad Info laughs from the pews.

Trust me, you don't want to be that cousin.

BUILDING OUT OUR STORIES

In her TED talk, "The Danger of a Single Story," storyteller and activist Chimamanda Ngozi Adichie famously states, "The problem with stereotypes is not that they aren't true, but they are incomplete. They make one story become the only story."[(1)]

Single stories are always incomplete. Yet, most of our stories—the ones we base whole-ass identities on—are single stories. Therefore, they too are incomplete. Sometimes, our single stories about people and places come from images we see on the news. Sometimes, they're built on one perspective shared by Someone of Importance and then mimicked by those that person has influenced. Sometimes we assign a belief or trait to a macro population based on a micro experience.

Many years ago, my friend Bobby was jumped outside a club in Providence, Rhode Island. The assailants were Black men. This story caused him to unconsciously assign the capacity for violence he'd experienced from those three individuals to all Black men.

---

(1) https://www.youtube.com/watch?v=D9Ihs241zeg

At work, he began encountering kind, intelligent Black professionals and wasn't sure how to respond. To ease his cognitive dissonance, he started referring to those particular Black men as "the good kind."

"How many fights have you been in in your life, Bobby?" I asked him.

"I don't know. Probably around ten."

"How many of those were with white men?"

"Most of them. I guess all of them but the one. Why?"

"I just think it's interesting that you didn't assign this capacity for violence to the white men you fought. Do you think it's because you identify as a white man and not a Black man?"

Thankfully, Bobby knows me, and so he got curious, not defensive. He later told me that our conversation hit him hard, and that it prompted him to reflect deeply on how he defined his world and where his stories came from. Humbled and a bit embarrassed, he began to show up more mindfully at work. His relationships with, and trust in, his Black colleagues changed for the better because he was willing to see that he'd been operating on Bad Info and it was time to change his story.

Not everyone is this open or self-aware. But if you want to un-funk your leadership and see immediate results with your team, you must be willing to examine your stories.

IS YOUR INTELLECT DRUNK AT THE BBQ?

The ASJs are cousins to identity in that they're directly attached to identity's narrow parameters. Separately, they're problematic. Together—especially when fueled by uncertainty, fear, insecurity, laziness, self-loathing, and Bad Info—they're an intellectually and professionally fatal combination.

Here's one way this plays out in leadership spaces.

My friend Sloane is a brilliant writer, scholar, and professor. She's warm and engaging and tells sing-songy stories in her lilting Irish accent. She's earned two PhDs, one in Global Histories and the other in Ancient Religions, and is a wealth of fascinating history, knowledge, insight, and perspective.

Yet, when people first meet her, they're often surprised by her demeanor, intellect, and wit. Her wild black curls, piercing upturned blue eyes, full-sleeve tattoos, and multiple piercings give many people pause. She looks scary. She looks intimidating. She looks like [insert negative stereotype about grunge-era kids here]. Her graduate students are often confused when she takes the podium.

If you just thought, "Well, what the hell does she expect? If she wants to be perceived as an intellectual, she should present herself that way," hold that thought.

Sloane was recently approached via email to present at a symposium after an Important Person at the university read a scholarly article that she'd published. He enthusiastically expressed that he found her work "riveting" and "groundbreaking" when they spoke on the phone and agreed to meet via video to plan her presentation. He hoped, he stated, that it would be "keynote-worthy."

During their video chat, Sloane noted that he was less enthusiastic, almost withdrawn. He kept saying things like, "If you find you are unable to make the symposium, we can find a replacement."

She inquired about this marked difference and, after an

awkward pause and a haughty inhale, was told that her appearance was "surprising" and there was a concern about audience engagement.

"My appearance does not diminish my intellect and expertise on the subject matter," Sloane reminded him. "You would be doing yourself, your audience, and me a grave disservice to exclude my research and this information from the university's symposium."

In the end, she did deliver a keynote at the symposium, and her presentation was incredibly well-received.

Sloane's story worked out in part because of her willingness to point out that Mr. Important Person's ASJs were bumbling around in full view. But so many other talented, knowledgeable people never even have a chance.

Maybe you, too, have avoided or overlooked people because of the assumptions you've made about them, or because they fit stereotypes that you've believed.

Or, maybe, like Sloane, you've been overlooked because you "didn't look the part"—or, worse, were blatantly judged based on your gender expression, skin color, religion, assumed religion, accent, fashion choices, or something else.

Or maybe, like many of us, you've experienced both.

Assumptions, stereotypes, and judgments are patterned behaviors rooted in ignorance, fear, and, dare I say, laziness. That sounds mean, but it's true. Too often, we just take Bad Info as gospel without doing our research or looking for opportunities to have our own direct experience. ASJs are the antithesis of mindfulness—allowing awareness to arise by paying attention—and ASJ behavior is the intellectual and emotional equivalent of being the drunk uncle at the family barbecue.

So, if you thought Sloane should have presented herself differently in order to avoid triggering ASJ behavior from others, my question to you is, "Why?" To whose standards of "professional" should she aspire? What value does that actually bring? Does her appearance truly matter more than her intellect and subject matter expertise? Why should a person expressing themselves through their appearance trigger so much insecurity and judgment?

And, if you dismissed others' judgments of her by saying, "What does she expect?" Well, this kind of thinking tiptoes us into larger, more dangerous societal postures, like, "What was she wearing?" and "Why did he have his hood up? He looked like a threat."

Yup, ASJ behavior is not only intellectually fatal, sometimes, it can be physically fatal.

So, let's play a word association game.

UN-FUNK YOUR ASJs

Jot down the first three or four descriptors that come to mind when you read the words below. Use a journal or download the workbook at **www.unfunkyourselfbook.com**.

Autistic	**Criminal**	**The South**
Terrorist	**Teacher**	**Homeless**
Airline Pilot	**Democrat**	**Gen-X**
Drug Dealer	**Immigrant**	**CEO**
Millennial	**Welfare**	**New England**
Gun violence	**American**	**Republican**
Healthy	**Professor**	**Housekeeper**
Successful	**Happy**	**European**
Depression	**Africa**	**Police Officer**

Then, for each word and set of descriptors, go back and ask yourself these questions:

- Is this true?
- No, really. Is this true?
- Is it a complete understanding?
- Have I ever directly experienced this thing?
- What do I think I know?
- Why do I think I know it?
- What do I know I don't know?
- What might I not know that I haven't thought about?
- How will I gather more information?

What did you discover about your thoughts and knowledge on these topics?

As you went through this exercise, did you catch yourself leaning into any ASJs? If you did, that's normal. But, if you did, how did you catch yourself, and how did you think about them?

We don't know everything about everything. Most of us don't know everything about even *one* thing. Though your primal brain would disagree, it's okay to not know everything; your logical brain should be on board with that. It's okay to want to learn, too.

As a leader, you aren't *supposed* to know everything. That's an impossible standard to hold yourself to, and it's rooted in fear. Accept that you know what you know, and that you know some of what you don't know. Further, accept that there are many things you don't know that you don't know—and that, as a human, you might launch into your ASJs when presented with those things.

To be a mindful, effective leader, it's imperative to examine your single stories, assumptions, and stereotypes, and to keep your judgment in check. So, when you run into those things that you didn't know you didn't know, instead of creating a story that satisfies your primal brain, be curious and seek every angle of the truth, even if that means leaning into some discomfort.

CHAPTER SIX

EQ: THE ULTIMATE LEADERSHIP CHEAT CODE

JOY, AN OFFICE MANAGER in a State Department office, wished good morning to Liz, a senior staff member, in the hallway one morning. Liz didn't respond and kept walking to her office.

Slightly stunned and offended, Joy went to her desk and complained to Ann, the other office manager. "I think Liz is mad at me. She just ignored me in the hallway."

At the same time Joy and Ann were talking, Alan walked into the office and asked how they were. Ann replied, "Good, except that Liz is mad at Joy today."

"What? Why?"

"I don't know," Joy shrugged. "She just ignored me in the hallway for no reason. It was so rude!"

Much of the staff was filing into the office now. Alan made an offhand comment to James, his colleague, to "stay away from Liz this morning. Seems like she's having a bad day already."

James, who works closely with Liz, went into Liz's office. "Hey, Liz. Everything okay?"

Liz was taken aback. "Totally fine. Why?"

"Well, Joy said you ignored her in the hallway this morning.

She thinks you're mad at her."

"James, I had my earbuds in. I was watching my niece's graduation videos on my phone since I couldn't be there in person. I didn't even hear Joy say good morning."

Liz then marched straight out into the office and confronted Joy. "Next time you think I'm mad at you, just ask me, okay?"

Joy apologized, but now Liz really *was* mad at her, and the whole day was tense for everyone because of it. And it all started because Joy lacked the emotional intelligence to ask for clarification before enrolling the entire office in her personal discomfort. A quick conversation with Liz could have cleared up the whole misunderstanding, but instead, she convinced the entire staff that what she was feeling was true, accurate, and totally justified—and that they should also act on this information.

Drama, anyone?

THE SECRET SAUCE OF LEADERSHIP

Emotional intelligence is a complex topic that we'll digest in pieces and parts. This is the part of the book during which the work gets real, y'all. And if you made a face when I mentioned emotional intelligence back in Chapter One ... well, put on your swimmies, because we're diving right into the deep end.

According to Psychology Today, emotional intelligence (EQ) is "the ability to identify and manage one's own emotions, as well as the emotions of others."[(1)]

High emotional intelligence is one of those "soft skills"

---

(1) https://www.psychologytoday.com/us/basics/emotional-intelligence

that make successful leaders successful. It's not a "nice to have." It's a must. Luckily, like most skills, emotional intelligence can be trained and developed. And it begins with—you guessed it—mindfulness.

A high level of emotional intelligence is necessary to identify and name your own emotions and manage them well. All the theory and discussion we've explored across the previous three chapters has been building up to this. Intellect is the gateway to understanding, but understanding our feelings is the path to growth.

If you can name your truest, deepest emotions, you can control them. Better, you can apply them to tasks like critical and creative thinking, problem-solving, engaging an audience effectively, and navigating the various ups and downs of professional and personal relationships.

The four components of emotional intelligence are:

- Self-awareness
- Self-management
- Social awareness
- Relationship management

In this chapter, we will unpack and organize the four components of emotional intelligence so you can understand where you are, why you feel the way you do, and how to grow your emotional intelligence. Developing emotional intelligence is not a linear process, rather it's spherical thinking; it shifts, changes, and challenges you with each new experience. However, it always comes from the inside out. The process will require that you make space to be calm and mindful, present with your thoughts and emotions, and *non-judgmental* about what you're feeling and the myriad roots of those emotions.

Remember, judgment leads to shame, and shame leads to suffering.

So, before we move on, let's talk about shame.

We don't do shame here. What we *do* do is gentle analysis, personal growth, self-compassion, and gratitude for the chance to learn about ourselves, no matter how much it sucks in the moment. Why gratitude? Because every time we learn about ourselves, we have the chance to take action on what we learn, and become better leaders, better parents, better spouses, and better people all around.

Emotional intelligence isn't something most of us learned growing up, or even in our leadership training. In many cases, we've been taught to "leave that touchy-feely stuff at home, because leadership takes grit! *Grr!*" Sure, leadership takes grit—aka, perseverance and resilience—but it also takes flexibility, grace, and the ability to adapt. Without some soft, sticky mortar to hold it together, grit crumbles under pressure.

If leadership is a burger, emotional intelligence is the "secret sauce." Without it, the whole mess just doesn't hang together the same way.

Even though the benefits of emotional intelligence are well-known and extensively researched, many of us still call ourselves out for emotional thinking—or for feeling, well, anything. When we notice ourselves doing Bad Boss things or being generally mindless, our first reaction can be to try to shame ourselves into doing better. That isn't grit. That's grime.

If your best friend spoke to you the way your inner voice does, would you still be friends? Probably not. So, if you're telling yourself, "You're too stupid for this job," "Everyone knows you're a fraud," "Your staff is only nice to you because you're the boss. They don't actually like you," or "You're lucky to even *have* a job, so shut up!"—well, you've been hanging out with those nasty ASJs again, and it's time to kick those cousins out of the party.

Shame is not a productive motivator, internally or externally. Sure, you can use it to drive a temporary, fear-based reaction, but there's always a painful backlash. It will never bring you to a place of greater emotional awareness, only greater emotional turmoil.

You can probably recall a time when a Bad Boss used humiliation as a management tactic, whether privately or in front of your peers. If you're anything like me, you tucked your tail between your legs and tried to hold your head high as you shame-walked back to your desk to cry. When confronted, most of us want to appease the person in power, so we double down on "doing good work" until the emotional fog lifts and we become angry at being shamed.

Shame from leaders can be overt, like, "My dog could do better work than this," "How many times do I have to tell you this before you actually remember?" "Are you going to do it right this time?" or "Clearly, you're not capable of doing The Thing." Or, it might be sneaky, like, "Given your last performance review, I expected your numbers to be higher this time. Please explain what happened." Depending on the tone of voice in which they were delivered, these neutral words could feel curious and open or totally shaming. Unfortunately, most emotionally unintelligent bosses think that using nice words will mask their disdain.

Newsflash: it doesn't.

What was your response to being shamed? How did it make you feel? Were you motivated or scared?

Statements like those above don't *teach,* and they sure don't inspire. They simply degrade and demean, which is counterproductive to creating a culture of learning and growth. In fact, after hearing the above, most folks' initial reaction will be figuring out how to GTFO of this toxic place ASAP.

So, what do you think happens when you use humiliation on yourself, in your own head? You want to escape—which is the exact opposite of mindfulness. Using shame and humiliation as a tactic, whether on ourselves or others, is an emotional brain response, and *comes from your own self-worth issues.*

When I said earlier to approach this work calmly, gently, and above all, *non-judgmentally,* it's not because I want to turn you into a weepy snowflake who needs to be bottle-fed and cosseted. It's because *shame doesn't work.*

Now that we've covered that, let's move on to shadows, masks, and mirrors—aka, the basics of emotional intelligence.

#1: SELF-AWARENESS

After a suicide attempt, Adam, a former colleague of mine, spent a few days in a psychiatric hospital exploring the roots of his incredible hopelessness. To anyone looking at him, his life was pretty much perfect. He was married to a lovely woman with whom he shared two adorable kids. He held a fantastic job as a public servant, lived in a desirable neighborhood, and was surrounded by loving family. On the surface, he had nothing to be sad about—certainly nothing so terrible that he should try to take his own life.

What Adam acknowledged during his intense and heavily-medicated hospital stay was that he is, and always has been, gay. But he knew that his conservative Catholic family would not just disapprove, they would disown him. To avoid this pain, he didn't just shove his true sexual orientation into the proverbial closet, he burned it, chopped it up, stuck it in a box, and buried it in the basement. Then, he donned the persona of a straight man like a new suit and set about living his life.

Only, as we know, nothing in our inner boxes stays buried forever. His self-denial was like poison leaking into his psyche.

Prior to Adam's shadow revelation, he was an active and outspoken critic of the LGBTQ+ community, loudly opposing same-sex marriage and adoption, appearing on radio talk shows, and even testifying before the State legislature. He referred to the LGBTQ+ community as "morally corrupt" and "blasphemous," stating that anyone who didn't conform to straight, cisgender norms was destined for Hell and deserved to burn for their sins.

I can't even imagine how it must have felt for Adam to not only have his private life revealed as a facade, but also his public platform. But in the end, even that shame was preferable to the dissonance between his persona and his shadow; the pain, even when it was still subconscious, was so immense that he would rather end his life than face it.

After lots of therapy and many hard discussions, Adam is living as himself—as a gay man with a family and a same-sex partner. He has issued numerous public apologies to the LGBTQ+ community for his prior attacks. His ex-wife has been incredibly supportive of him throughout this entire process, and they are a great example to their community of how families with kids can navigate this kind of revelation.

Unfortunately, Adam's parents, aunts, and uncles were not so understanding. When he announced that he was gay, they fulfilled his greatest fear and cut him—and his wife and kids—out of their lives. But after a while, a few started to come around. It's not perfect, and there's still a lot of resentment on both sides, but they are putting in the work to heal together.

Today, Adam is the most content and fulfilled he's ever been. As a leader, he's now able to access and display a level of empathy that was completely unavailable to him before. People trust him more, and many even confide in him about their own mental health struggles. All the respect and admiration he wanted to command by "faking it" is now his, and he's not taking it lightly.

The first step in being a mindful leader to your employees is to first be a mindful leader to yourself.

That's right. You've got to lead *you* before you can lead *them.*

So, how do you become more self-aware? Well, first, you need to identify what you're actually feeling—which is harder than it seems.

Surface emotions are not full emotions, so when you're feeling a certain way, you will need to learn to excavate the root emotion and its reason. For example, if you feel resentment toward your boss or a coworker, that resentment has an emotional root of anger. So, the question then becomes, "What am I angry about, and where does that anger come from?" For example, if you're resentful because your new boss was hired from outside the team when you wanted to be promoted, you're probably angry about being passed over. Which boils down to you assuming that those doing the hiring don't think you're worthy of getting the job.

Check out this handy infographic by Abby VanMuijen[(2)]. It's important to note that emotions and feelings are not linear; they're often layered and ramble into each other. Root emotions are at the center of the circle, while their various expressions are in the outer rings.

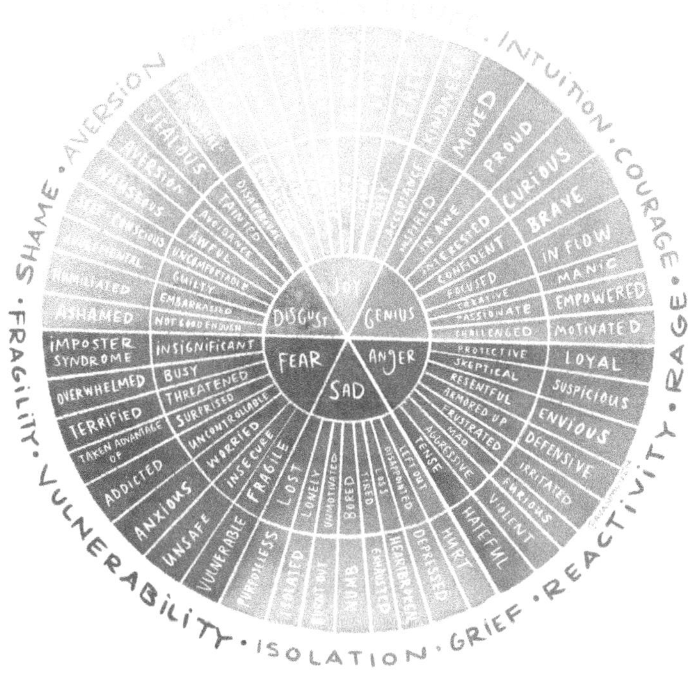

When examining how you feel about anything, you will need to explore the roots of your feelings. These are tied directly to your whole self and your whole truth—not the part

(2) https://www.avanmuijen.com

of you that you display outwardly, but also what you attempt to hide from the world by stuffing it in your attic or burying it in your basement.

According to Carl Jung, the famous Swiss psychiatrist and psychoanalyst who founded analytical psychology, every "persona" also has a "shadow." These elements represent different aspects of the human psyche. Each is necessary and contributes to a more comprehensive understanding of the whole person.

So, let's look deeper.

The Persona

The persona is the social mask or character that we wear outwardly so that we are more socially acceptable and interactive.

The persona is shaped by societal expectations, standards, and norms related to gender roles, sexuality, culture, race, ability, and class. These norms shape how we adapt and identify, resulting in broader patterns in our shadow and associated persona—such as women carrying the mental load for the household, and men not being allowed to cry.

Of course, we're not just shaped by society at large. Our home life and upbringing have a much greater impact as we take on the values, beliefs, and expectations of our parents and caregivers.

The persona is not the true self; rather, it is a facade built to conform to social standards in order to protect the ego from negative judgments and criticism. However, as Adam discovered, adopting a persona as a means of conforming can create sometimes catastrophic conflict with your true feelings and desires as well as your emotional, mental, and physical needs.

The Shadow

The shadow is an unconscious part of the psyche that contains the feelings and desires that we fear are socially unacceptable. We unconsciously reject these bits of our truth, along with our wounded self and wounded inner child, and shove them away into the dark corners of our mind so that we can conform to societal expectations.

We can't just get rid of or ignore our shadow, any more than we can avoid casting a shadow when we stand in the sun. We can try to shove it into the attic, but as soon as we're not paying attention it will jump out and mess with our sense of self. Our shadow can show up in emotional outbursts, self-destructive behaviors, relationship problems, substance abuse, and more. That's why it's essential to acknowledge and integrate the shadow into our conscious awareness; when we know what's in the boxes, we can deal with it more mindfully, and even use it to our advantage. This process is called "shadow work."

Many people feel ashamed or guilty about their shadow because society or their upbringing has taught them to feel that way. Social norms, power dynamics, and identity concepts heavily influence many of our natural and learned behaviors. From the first time we cry, laugh, or speak, the feedback we get affects whether we keep doing those things. Our developing brains can predict outcomes, like how a caregiver might react negatively to something we do. This foresight can lead us to suppress our natural behaviors, which can build up as repression over time.

As we grow up, our shadow affects our behavior just as much as our behavior shapes the shadow. When we ignore and quash the shadow, it creates a detrimental feedback loop between our conscious and unconscious mind. The more we hide and avoid our natural tendencies, the more parts of ourselves we lock away. This only makes the shadow grow stronger and more extensive.

The shadow isn't just about the "worst" parts of ourselves (because "worst" is relative and based on how we define "bad," which is based on our conditioning and often a whole bunch of ASJs). It can also include repressed trauma, unmet needs, and even interests that others deem socially unsuitable. Displaying "weird" interests or discussing traumatic experiences is often taboo, leading to self-blame and shame. We learn to detest our shadow, seeing it as an enemy—which ultimately messes with our ability to accept ourselves, which in turn messes with our ability to connect with and love others.

And, for any neurospicy folks—fellow ADHDers, autistic kindred, and other neurodivergent friends—there's a whole other layer to all of this. We often mask our symptoms, habits and needs around others, even our families. Vocal and physical stims and sensory triggers are involuntary and can't be turned off, but the social pressure to hide them is *so* strong. Quelling those needs creates stress from the shadow, and generates real psychological discomfort, anxiety, and exhaustion, so it's important to honor your sensory needs and to be honest about them. Though your stims and triggers are no one's business, it's helpful if you can explain them in an overarching manner. For example, overhead lights are incredibly bothersome to me (especially fluorescents—I can hear them buzz and that drives me nuts!), so I request table and/or floor lamps in my office space. Perhaps you need to walk around when you're brainstorming as that helps you process. Perhaps you need to tap your feet when you're typing. Whatever it is, gently mention your need and then just do it. Most people will not care; rather, they will work to ensure you're comfortable. Humans are wired for connection. When we find connection points, like being able to care for others, we dial in that connection.

Internal Conflict, Projection, and Emotional Chaos

Internal conflict occurs when the persona suppresses aspects of the true self that are considered unacceptable by societal standards and relegates them to the shadow. When that happens, the propensity to be controlled by rogue emotions is hella-high.

It's crucial to achieve a balance between your persona and your shadow by recognizing the shadow's influence. This allows you to authentically express yourself instead of masking all the time. So, like, please stop pretending everything is fine when it's not, find the courage to confide your worries and fears in your trusted friends and family, and be brave enough to be yourself even if you fear that others might think you're "weird" or "bad." Let that shit go. Mindfully.

When this balance of persona and shadow is uneven, people will often compensate by projecting the disdain they hold for their own shadow onto others who possess those "undesirable" traits. This is what happened to Adam. His shadow was so strong that it ended up harming not only him, but also others that his words and actions oppressed, minimized, and attacked.

For most of us, the projection of our shadow isn't quite so blatant, but it can be every bit as harmful. Joy, whose story I shared at the start of this chapter, probably had a whole lot of "worthless" and "not good enough" hiding in her attic boxes. When Liz unknowingly walked by without saying hello, Joy's shadow came roaring out and upset the emotional stability of the whole office.

Un-funking yourself and your leadership approach requires that you be the Big Boss of your emotions. Being controlled by rogue emotions hidden in your shadow is a super funked-up way to be, especially when you're trying to lead other people who may be controlled by their own rogue emotions.

I'm not going to ask you to make friends with your shadow, although that is the ultimate goal. I am asking that you begin to see and understand your shadow so you know when it's rearing its sad, scared little head, and give it some love before it spirals out of control.

Below are some tips and tricks to gaining control over your emotions, even the really big ones, and keeping your shadow in check.

- *Name it to tame it.* Identify what you're feeling. Is it rage, sadness, or misalignment—or are you just hangry? Then, journal it. The more energy you give to taming the emotion, the more quickly you will gain control.
- *Find the "why."* Understand the source of your feelings. Was it really that email that annoyed you, or are you upset about something else and just projecting? Are you snapping at your kids when it's really your spouse who's annoying you?

- *Analyze, analyze.* Examine your reactions. Why did you react the way you did? Was it level with the issue at hand, or was it an overreaction? Where did you learn to react the way you did?

Understanding how to tame your emotions will help you gain insight into your behaviors and motivations, leading to a more integrated and holistic sense of self.

Once you acknowledge and accept your shadow, your emotional awareness will increase dramatically, as will your self-compassion. You'll also be better equipped to manage your emotions, demonstrate empathy, build confidence, and generate strong relationships at work, at home, and across the board.

So, now that you understand what self-awareness actually entails, how do you go about excavating your shadow and creating more balance between it and your persona?

Brilliant question! I have compiled a comprehensive list of guiding questions that will help you excavate your shadow parts and define them non-judgmentally.

Take your time, answering the following questions thoughtfully and honestly. No one is going to see this but you. There is no deadline, and you may find yourself revisiting the questions with more information as you allow yourself to learn more about your shadow.

Once you've finished answering the questions on the next page, you can explore the shadow work resources at **www.unfunkyourselfbook.com** to continue your journey.

- How do you define failure?
- Where did you learn that definition of failure?
- How do you navigate failure?
- What does conflict mean to you?
- How do you navigate conflict?
- Where did you learn to navigate conflict like that?
- How do you handle times of uncertainty?
- What is your greatest fear?
- Why are you afraid of that particular thing?
- What were taboo topics in your household when you were growing up?
- What are the traits of the people you admire most?
- What are the traits of the people you dislike the most?
- What traits are you most critical of related to colleagues and employees?
- What behavior do you judge yourself the most for?
- What behaviors do you believe are disrespectful?
- What discoveries have you made so far in this exercise?

Journaling vs Diary Writing

What we're doing here is not a "Dear Diary" exercise. You're not using the page as a repository for all of your funked-up thoughts, or writing to justify or confirm your own feelings. Journaling is deliberate self-reflection and a problem-solving activity that helps you find calm in the midst of chaos. It's also great for creative thinking, critical thinking, and making plans to (lovingly and mindfully) take over the world. Further, it's space to cultivate and demonstrate gratitude, which is a fantastic foundation to begin shifting into a more mindful way of existing.

Here's how to journal mindfully.

- *Use a pen/pencil and paper.* We tend to emotionally focus better when we're writing than when we're typing. It's a body/mind thing.
- *Minimize distractions.* Remember that distraction bit we talked about earlier? If you want to get the most out of your journaling time, ditch your phone and find a place where you can focus and do the thing.
- *Don't worry about "formatting."* There are no rules to journaling. Do you want to write? Doodle? Rhyme? Illustrate? Use bullet points? It's really whatever floats your boat as long as you're doing it mindfully and with full presence.

- *Make it a habit.* The simplest way to do this is to attach it to a daily habit you already have—like sitting with your coffee in the morning or drinking a cup of tea before bed in the evening. This is called "habit stacking." I like sitting in bed with my under-eye patches and Whitestrip on while I write. Let it replace scrolling through socials. The "right" time is up to you based on your schedule and your emotional availability.

Self-Aware vs Self-Conscious

I've been asked in workshops if being self-aware and being self-conscious are the same thing. Though they're related, there's a huge difference between self-consciousness and self-awareness.

Self-awareness refers to recognizing the different aspects of your individuality, such as emotions, values, needs, and desires. When you are self-aware, you seek internal validation (rather than external) and honor what you specifically need to function well within yourself, in your relationships, and in society. Self-awareness is often associated with feelings of inner peace, validation, and fulfillment.

Self-consciousness, on the other hand, is rooted in external validation, deep fears, and others' judgments. It can mean being excessively concerned about your appearance or manner, seeking validation from authority figures, friends, or the internet, and feeling constantly ashamed and embarrassed. If you're self-conscious, you might struggle with timidity, low self-esteem, decreased confidence, jealousy, anxiety, depression, and/or paranoia.

Mindfulness practices lead to more self-awareness and less self-consciousness. When you know who you are and you honor that truth, the need for external validation as a measure of worth and means of acceptance diminishes. The imposter syndrome fades, jealousy weakens, and confidence rises. It's kind of a win-win.

Don't forget to download your shadow work journal at **www.unfunkyourselfbook.com**!

#2: SELF-MANAGEMENT

It's really hard to manage and control your behavior when you aren't aware of the behavior in the first place.

Self-management begins with self-awareness and involves developing and maintaining habits and strategies to control your thoughts, emotions, and behaviors effectively. A lack of self-management (which is usually accompanied by a lack of self-awareness) can create minor dramas like the one Joy started, or major life and relationship upheavals. Either way, poor self-management isn't a good look for anyone who wants to lead effectively.

Here are some steps to help you practice self-management:

- *Identify your triggers.* Understand what situations or people trigger strong emotional reactions in you and why.
- *Recognize your emotions.* What are the emotions you are feeling, and how strong are they? Name them to tame them.

- *Reframe your lens.* Challenge and reframe your thoughts. Check to make sure you're not operating off assumptions, stereotypes, or Bad Info. Examine your judgments without trying to justify them.
- *Delay your reaction.* When you feel a strong emotion, pause before responding. Count to ten, take a few deep breaths, or step away from the situation if possible. There is nothing at all wrong with saying, "Let me think about that and get back to you," or "Pardon me, could you clarify what you meant so I make sure I understand?"

Managing your emotions (after becoming aware of your emotions) mitigates reactive tendencies and supports responsive, thoughtful ones, which allows you to remain calm. In tense situations, a calm leader is the best leader.

#3: SOCIAL AWARENESS

Social awareness is a critical component of emotional intelligence and plays a vital role in building healthy relationships, fostering collaboration, and creating inclusive environments in both personal and professional contexts. It helps individuals navigate social interactions more effectively and contributes to the overall well-being of communities.

Social awareness encompasses several key components:

- *Read the room.* Recognize and correctly interpret verbal and nonverbal cues.
- *Take in others' perspectives.* Attempt to see situations from others' viewpoints.
- *Appreciate diversity.* Genuinely value different backgrounds, cultures, and perspectives.
- *Communicate effectively.* Foster clear, respectful exchanges with others that take into account their viewpoints and emotional states.
- *Cultivate empathy.* Understand and share the feelings of another person.

We'll tackle communication skills, perspectives, and diversity a bit later in this book. What's really important for our purposes here is empathy—what it is, what it isn't, and how to apply it effectively.

Empathy is the most useful of the Big Four Emotional Responses—the other three being sympathy, apathy, and disdain. So, let's define all of these.

Sympathy

Sympathy is feeling pity or sorrow for someone. We send sympathy cards to friends when they lose loved ones. We sympathize with people who are going through something we've been through, like a twisted ankle or a tough breakup. Sympathy can have a spurious feel to it, too, especially if we feel uncomfortable with a certain conversation.

According to researcher and author Brené Brown, if you

find yourself using the phrase "at least," you are practicing spurious sympathy. For example, "At least you only broke your toe, and not your ankle." Or "At least you got a severance package when they laid you off."

Comparative suffering falls into this category as well, and it looks something like this.

Coworker: "I'm totally overwhelmed at work and my boss won't do anything to help me reduce my workload!"

You: "Well, at least you *have* a job. Fifty people in my department got laid off last year."

Apathy

Apathy is a lack of interest or concern related to others' feelings, perspectives, and experiences. When you're apathetic, you just don't care about whatever the other person is telling you.

Coworker: "Our policies don't address the rising mental health issues we're seeing in the office."

You: "That doesn't affect me, so I don't really care."

Disdain

Disdain is the sister of contempt. We feel disdain when we believe someone or something is unworthy of consideration. We may even have a visceral response to a person or situation.

Coworker: "I'm totally overwhelmed at work and my boss won't do anything to help me reduce my workload!"

You (probably in your head): "Well, maybe you should toughen up there, buttercup, and get on with it like the rest of us do."

Empathy

Empathy is the act of being genuinely curious, honestly listening to and believing someone's story (even if their story makes absolutely no sense to your identity and to your experiences), and then using that understanding to guide your subsequent actions.

Empathy is what unites humans. Empathy is what vanquishes political and social division. Empathy is what allows us to forgive and move past grudges into a place of acceptance and inner peace.

Empathy is a superpower.

Often, empathy is described as the ability to "walk in another person's shoes." On the surface that makes sense, but there is a fundamental flaw in this concept. Because of our identities and the biases, assumptions, and judgments therein, it is impossible to walk in the shoes of a person with whom you don't identify. And, because of that, when we try to walk in those shoes, it's often through a lens of sympathy (pity), apathy, or disdain. For example, it's impossible for me to "walk in the shoes" of a Black trans woman. I have absolutely no idea what being a Black trans woman feels like. I have no practical knowledge of that existence and, if I were not mindful, I might hold some sort of well-meaning pity for the Black trans community. *Eww.* Trans women don't need pity. They deserve empathy, just like literally everyone else on the planet.

Here's what empathy looks like using the examples above.

- **Coworker:** "I'm totally overwhelmed at work and my boss won't do anything to help me reduce my workload!"

- **You:** "What has happened at work to create such an overwhelming situation for you? What does your boss say about the overwhelm?"
- **Coworker:** "Our policies don't address the rising mental health issues we're seeing in the office."
- **You:** "Before we address policies, we need to understand the culture dynamics."

Empathy is not easy to practice, especially when it comes to people who have hurt us, humiliated us, disdained us, ignored us, or just plain pissed us off. Remember Miranda, my Bad Boss from Chapter One? Working for her was *impossible,* and I spent a long time holding on to the pain, humiliation, and anger of that experience. Any time I thought about that job I would have a visceral reaction. My mental fists would go up, and I'd immediately go into my emotional brain. Honestly, even now, when I wrote the story to use in this book, I felt the familiar "zing" of uncomfortable emotion. So, I sat with it for a moment, allowing the anger to serve its purpose. Then, I reminded myself that the experience was a huge lesson. More, it couldn't have been easy to be Miranda. She was open about her bipolar disorder, and even more open about her abhorrence of psychotropic medication. She had a horrifyingly abusive childhood and built her nonprofit because she had first-hand experience with the needs she served. Knowing her story doesn't excuse her actions, or lessen their impact, but it does help me find empathy for her.

Sympathy, Apathy, and Disdain Are Empathy Blockers

My longtime friend Cliff, an incredibly bright and hilarious engineer, talented guitarist and drummer, renowned D&D Dungeon Master, and *Star Trek* nerd extraordinaire, has lived a disrupted and difficult life since 2012 when he developed an addiction to opioids.

Addiction is messy on many levels. Many people blame the addict for "getting themselves into this situation" and provide all sorts of criticisms, judgments, and well-meaning (or not so well-meaning) advice. Addiction is one area where sympathy, apathy, and disdain combine with assumptions, stereotypes, and judgments to create an emotional toxic sludge that helps no one and hurts everyone.

Sympathy offers pity and looks to provide "help" in the form of either advice or toxic positivity. "Just go to rehab and you'll get better!" We feel like, if we provide a solution, we've done our job and can move along. Now, the yucky situation is their problem, not ours. As Brené Brown reminds us, "Help is the sunny side of control."

Cliff has been to rehab. Seven times, in fact. Addiction changes a person's brain chemistry so that the chemical or substance is now required for normal functioning, even after the body has detoxed. Rehab programs, though they can help people "dry out" or detox, are not always helpful in the long term, especially for alcohol and opioids.

There's a saying in the substance recovery world: "The road to recovery is paved with relapse." In Cliff's case, this has been very true. After his sixth rehab stay, he remained sober for four years—right up until his father passed away and the stress of managing the aftermath became too much. We almost lost Cliff to an overdose that time.

Which brings me to apathy.

Apathy says, "I can't do this anymore. I'm done"—and deserts the relationship. The discomfort and frustration associated with being an addict's friend or relative can become overwhelming. Caring for a person with an addiction can feel like an emotional liability. In certain cases, it can even be a physical danger. Apathy like this sits on the other side of sympathy. It comes after you've given the advice, researched the rehabs, called the right help lines … and watched the same story play out over and over. You've tried to help, but it hasn't worked, and you feel like this whole situation is just toxic to your system and you need to get out.

Maybe you even feel that the person themselves is toxic—and that's where we move into disdain.

Disdain also sits on the other side of sympathy but is more aggressive and reactive. The disdainful people in Cliff's life were furious that he relapsed. They called him a failure, and loudly proclaimed that if he hadn't gotten himself into this mess in the first place, everything would be fine. Disdain layers shame on top of the existing pain.

What's important to note for our purposes is that all three of these responses—sympathy, apathy, and disdain—stem from expectations and the emotions that arise when those expectations are not met. We expect that, when we provide a solution, the solution should be accepted, and that should be that. Anything else creates frustration and discomfort.

The expectation for Cliff was to "just get better already." Certainly, there was concern for his health, but the bigger feeling at play for most people in his life was their own discomfort: the discomfort of not having a quick fix (because we don't like ambiguity); the discomfort of being "stuck" in an uncomfortable emotional place with someone we love; the discomfort of feeling powerless to stop what is happening.

And then, there's empathy.

Empathy takes a bigger-picture view of a situation with no expectations. In Cliff's case, empathy asks, "How did you get here in the first place?"

Well, Cliff, like so many folks, ended up addicted after being prescribed opioids by his medical team after he was in a horrible motorcycle accident that crushed many of the bones on the left side of his body. He endured numerous surgeries, the pain of which was controlled via a fentanyl patch and oral Oxycontin. His body became dependent on the drugs, but per protocol, his physicians cut off access to the medicine after a certain number of weeks. There was no gradual reduction, no assisted detox period. One minute, he was on heavy-duty painkillers, and the next he was cut off. So, Cliff did what many (if not most) people would do in this case: he looked elsewhere for chemical relief.

Empathy is not condoning and it's not enabling. It's simply seeking understanding and adjusting your approach without pity, disdain, or expectations. You can empathetically set boundaries and/or leave a relationship because it doesn't serve you. The difference is that, when empathy is in the mix, you can do so without the backlash of shame.

Why am I using Cliff's story in a leadership book? Because I'm willing to bet that you know a bit about Cliff's struggle from first-hand personal experience. Maybe you've been addicted yourself, or still are. Maybe you've witnessed friends, family, or a partner struggle. And, even if neither of the above apply, I can guarantee that at least a handful of your coworkers struggle with addictions to drugs, alcohol, sex, gambling, shopping, or something else. I can also guarantee that, whether you know it or not, you're working with people who have crippling anxiety, depression, or bipolar disorder, and work hard to mask so they remain "acceptable."

We don't know everyone's stories, and they're not our business to know. But everyone has a story, and so many people are struggling with things we don't know about and might not understand even if we did know. So, instead of blaming people or falling into apathy and disdain to avoid the discomfort of their reality, lean into empathy. Try to understand the person in front of you with no expectations or requirements. Understand for the sake of understanding.

Every human being, including you, deserves the respect that is empathy. Judgment, disdain, and shame only serve to destroy. There is no productivity in them.

#4: RELATIONSHIP MANAGEMENT

Relationship management is the outward expression of our internal self and social awareness work. It's EQ in action.

Relationship management as a leader consists of, at the very least, how we communicate and how we navigate conflict. The next three chapters are a deep dive into this topic and will provide some solid assessment materials and how-tos for interacting with your teams, colleagues, and your own boss.

UN-FUNK YOUR EQ

The work gets a bit harder here. When you're ready, take some quiet time to consider the following questions related to each of these emotional responses.

Sympathy

- Think of a time when you felt sympathy for someone. How did you respond, and what did that experience teach you about caring for others?
- Is there a difference between sympathy and pity? Write about a moment when you confused the two.
- Have you ever received sympathy when you didn't want it? How did it make you feel, and why do you think that was?
- How does sympathy shape relationships? Reflect on how being sympathetic or receiving sympathy has affected your connections.

Apathy

- Write about a situation where you felt apathetic. What led to this feeling, and how did it impact your actions or relationships?
- Have you ever pretended to care about something you were really indifferent to? Why, and what was the outcome?

- Is apathy ever a useful response? Explore when, if ever, apathy might be a defense mechanism or a sign of burnout.
- What do you think apathy says about your current emotional state? Is there something deeper beneath your indifference?

Disdain

- Recall a time when you felt disdain for someone or something. What triggered it, and how did it shape your behavior?
- How do you typically deal with feelings of disdain? Write about whether you express it openly or keep it to yourself, and the impact that has.
- Can disdain ever be productive or helpful? Reflect on whether disdain ever motivates you to take action or improve a situation.
- How do you think others perceive you when you express disdain? Does it change their opinion of you?

Empathy

- Describe a moment when you truly empathized with someone. How did this change the way you interacted with them?

- What are the challenges of being empathetic? Write about the emotional toll it can take and how you manage it.
- Can you think of a time when your empathy for someone shifted your perspective on a situation? How did it alter your understanding or response?
- What practices help you become more empathetic in your everyday life? Reflect on how you can strengthen your ability to connect emotionally with others.

CHAPTER SEVEN

HOW YOU SAY WHAT YOU SAY, AND WHY IT MATTERS

MY FORMER COLLEAGUE, Kevin, had (in my opinion at the time) a habit of asking irrelevant questions and offering no substantive input in collaboration meetings.

During one meeting in which we and six other instructors and designers were modifying class curricula, he said, "Maybe we should have a conversation with the original author and find out what he meant by these slides."

It's important to note that the author's name is listed on the title page of the curriculum packet we were reviewing. I reminded Kevin that I, a woman, am the author, as indicated on the title page, and therefore we didn't require clarification. "We're just trying to use simpler language and less mumbo-jumbo for this next cohort of students," I said.

But Kevin asked the same question again—using the same language—as we reviewed other classes. Again, I reminded him that I, a woman (not "he"), am the author and we are just streamlining the information.

"Perhaps you could add some creative thought to the process?" I asked.

The third time he asked the exact same question, I snapped.

"Kevin, your persistent intellectual indifference is *infuriating*. Offer substantial suggestions or stop speaking." I rolled my eyes and glared at him. I was pissed off, heated up, and tired of dealing with this bullshit. I mean, why did he assume that the author *must* be a man? Why did he insist on it being a man *even after I told him I wrote the damn thing?* Not to mention how asinine it was to ask the same question three times and completely ignore the answer I was giving!

The gravity of my mistake hit me like a ton of bricks when Kevin did what anyone would do after being publicly humiliated. He rose quietly from his chair, eyes downcast, and left the room.

Oh, shit.

I was totally embarrassed to have behaved in such an unprofessional manner. Realizing how badly I'd embarrassed Kevin and that I'd hurt his feelings, I tumbled right into remorse. Wow. I was an asshole.

My colleagues were looking at the table, their papers, the ceiling … anywhere but at me. My boss finally raised her eyebrows and gestured toward the door. So, off I went to find Kevin, apologize, and bring him back to the table. Before I left, I apologized to the entire group for my unprofessional behavior.

Kevin was sitting at a table in the common space staring out the window. I approached the table slowly. "Kevin, I'm so sorry. That was completely unprofessional of me. Will you come back to the meeting? We don't want to go on without you there."

He nodded. "But you're right. I don't belong in there. I don't belong here at all."

The last of my frustration evaporated. I was obviously

missing something and was curious to learn his perspective.

Kevin explained that he is the first person in his family to have gone to college. Now he's working at a college—with instructors and designers, even. He had always longed to be a professor and a researcher, but now he felt like a fish out of water. "I feel like I have nothing to offer, but I don't want to be quiet, so I try to add something to these meetings even if it's small." He didn't even know that the author's info was on the first page of the packet.

I apologized again for being a total jerk. My judgment had fully transitioned into empathy. "My anger and frustration really had nothing to do with you or your actions," I admitted. "I can't tell you the number of times that men have questioned my intellect and ability as a woman in academia. When you referred to the author as 'he,' it just totally set me off because I received it as disrespectful. I projected my frustration onto you, which was not only unprofessional but completely unfair.

"I promise that I will never speak to you that way again, and that I will try to help guide you through this process and learn more about how this all works."

When we rejoined the table, I had a better understanding of Kevin's perspective. I apologized again to Kevin and to the entire room for my comments and demeanor. "I've also learned that I need to better explain the reason for curriculum changes and the process by which we vet new curricula so that our junior colleagues can have clarity and inclusion in the process."

There have been very few times in my life when I've been so embarrassed—and all because I let my outrage at a perceived insult take over and send me stumbling right into the mindless ASJ party.

The whole process lasted only about fifteen minutes, but it felt like a lifetime. We don't like to be wrong, and it's hard to admit mistakes and fault when we behave poorly. The ego wants to justify our actions, pass blame, and deflect liability to avoid admitting a mistake. The entire time I was talking with Kevin, apologizing to the group, and even for the rest of the meeting, my thoughts and emotions were running up and down the spectrum—from mad at myself for being an ass, mad at Kevin's questions, mad at men in general for not taking women seriously, all the way to genuine remorse and regret for the way I'd acted.

You might be thinking, "Kevin was wrong, too! If he didn't understand something, he should have just asked directly!" And you might be right. But as leaders, we can't control how other people communicate, or what they do or don't do. We can only control how *we* communicate, and from what mental and emotional state we choose to engage.

HOT ZONE, COOL ZONE

In Louise Evans's TEDx talk, "Own Your Behaviors, Master Your Communication,"[(1)] she illustrates different human behaviors using five different-colored chairs. I was inspired by this, and began to incorporate references to her talk into my workshops (with full credit, of course). But as time went on, I began to wonder if it's actually possible to be firmly in one "chair" at any given time. Human emotions are complex. We have the tendency to waffle and edge and feel multiple,

(1) https://www.youtube.com/watch?v=-KysuBl2m_w

sometimes conflicting, feelings at the same time.

Actually, it was my experience and behavior during the incident with Kevin that really got me thinking about this. And so, I created what I call "The Feedback Zone"—a sliding scale of behavior and responses that can help us identify when we are in a productive space to communicate and when to back off and chill the eff out.

So, buckle up, friend. You are about to enter another dimension—a dimension of not only sight and sound, but of a triggered amygdala. A journey into a spiral of feelings and emotional decisions. *Next stop: The Feedback Zone!*

(Okay, clearly I'm not Rod Serling, but you get the point. Now please go back and read that paragraph in your best Rod voice before proceeding.)

Every time we communicate with other people, we enter The Feedback Zone.

Every moment of every day, we are making choices about *how to behave* when we communicate. Do we choose sarcasm or sincerity? Kindness or "tough love"? Are we guarded and reactive, or are we open to receive feedback? Are we looking through only one lens or are we respecting differences of opinion? Are we needing to be "right"? Are we listening and speaking with empathy and emotional intelligence?

Every human loses their composure occasionally. Case in point: I don't regularly go around insulting the intellect of my colleagues—and in front of my boss, no less. Yet, I did it to Kevin, because his comments triggered my insecurities about being a woman in academia and sent me hurtling right into the Red Zone

THE FEEDBACK ZONE
RED ZONE
lashing out
blame/shame
losing control
"Screw you! It's all your fault!"
ORANGE ZONE
regret
internalized shame
justification
"I made a mistake"
YELLOW ZONE
lashing inward
self-punishment
fear of judgment
"I'm so ashamed"
GREEN ZONE
reframing assumptions
seeking perspective
"What's the whole picture here?"
TEAL ZONE
self-awareness
mindful reflection
"I'm feeling X because of Y experience/belief"
BLUE ZONE
setting boundaries with self and others
managing emotions
"What do I need, and how can I communicate that need respectfully?"
PURPLE ZONE
social awareness
mindfulness
"What does this person need and how can I get more info to support that respectfully?"
HOT ZONE
COOL ZONE

By the time Kevin asked his question for the third time, I was squarely in the Red Zone. Instead of doing what I needed to manage my emotional state, I opened my big mouth and all my ASJs came pouring out.

By the time Kevin left the room, I was in the Orange Zone: embarrassed, ashamed, grappling between "I was right" and "I'm sorry." But when my boss silently called me out, I slipped into Yellow: pure self-loathing.

This whole process took about fifteen seconds.

When I found Kevin out in the common area, I was still in the Yellow Zone, but when he told me, "I don't belong here," I shifted to Green and was able to pause and reflect. What was I missing?

As I listened to his side of the story, I scooted closer to Blue, and was able to gain some new perspective. Just as his questions and behavior had been born out of insecurity, so had my reaction. And, once that was off my chest, I stepped into the Purple Zone of social awareness.

Seems pretty linear, right? Nope. The minute I stepped back into the meeting room and saw all those faces, I slid right back over into Yellow for a hot minute. Only now, I had myself enough under control that I could progress with the meeting. For the rest of that day, I vacillated between Blue/Purple—self-compassion and empathy for Kevin—and Orange/Yellow. My ego wanted to justify what I had done and blame it on Kevin. My heart knew I was in the wrong and that I needed to accept responsibility.

My friend, *nothing productive* comes from the Hot Zone. When you lash out from a Red or Orange state, you may feel powerful for a minute, but in reality, you are sabotaging your leadership and giving away your power.

Think about a time a boss or colleague lost their temper, whether at you or at someone else. How highly did you think of them after that moment? How long did it take to trust them again?

My working relationship with Kevin took a hit that day, as did my relationship with every other person at that table. My assumption that Kevin was a slacker, the stereotype of "men don't respect women's achievements," and my judgment of his questions led to a snap reaction that damaged my professional reputation and put all of my future teaching assignments at risk.

Had I mindfully self-managed, I would have stepped away to feel my feelings and instead begun the conversation in the Green Zone. Asking Kevin why he kept asking the same question and how I could better define the process for him would have been a much better solution than insulting him. Had I done that, I would have understood that he was feeling vulnerable and uncomfortable, and as a leader, I would have adjusted to provide clarity and motivation. (And were he actually a slacker, I would have been able to shake that out using a Cool Zone logical process.)

I'm willing to guess that you've tripped in and out of the Hot Zones a few times, too. So, take a moment to mindfully reflect on your experiences. What were the results of those emotional eruptions? How can you handle it more productively next time?

GOOD RELATIONSHIP MANAGEMENT

Good interpersonal communication requires us to practice all aspects of emotional intelligence: self-awareness, self-management, social awareness, and relationship management. But what does good interpersonal communication look like? According to Albert Mehrabian, Professor Emeritus of Psychology at the University of California, Los Angeles, communication is mostly delivered and interpreted via nonverbal cues rather than spoken words.

Certainly, words, their meaning, and their delivery are important, but, according to his 55-38-7 rule, the bulk of how we deliver and receive information looks like this:

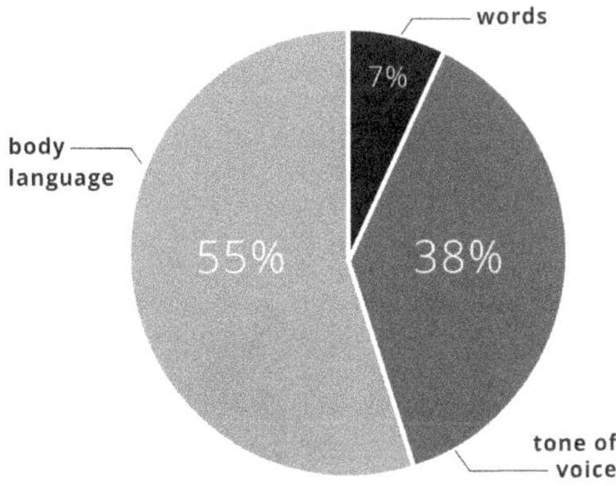

When people communicate in person, the three elements of the message—words, tone of voice, and body language—contribute differently to the impact of the message.

Effective communication requires that these three elements are compatible. If there is incongruence where the verbal and nonverbal cues contradict each other, the receiver might be confused or irritated by the conflicting messages.

So, what happens when we aren't able to interpret body language? Our brains still seek nonverbal input for clarification and intent of conversation. We pay a bit more attention to words, but really, we're listening to vocal quality—the tone, inflection, volume, pitch, and pace of speech.

I'm willing to bet that when you were younger, your parents often said something like, "Watch your tone with me, kid!"

Tone of voice lets the brain know the context of the conversation. Is it genuine, sarcastic, accusatory, compassionate?

Inflection likewise changes the meaning of a sentence based on the selected word. Here's an example sentence, "I have Metallica tickets."

I have Metallica tickets.

I *have* Metallica tickets.

I have *Metallica* tickets.

Same four words, three different intonations, three different meanings.

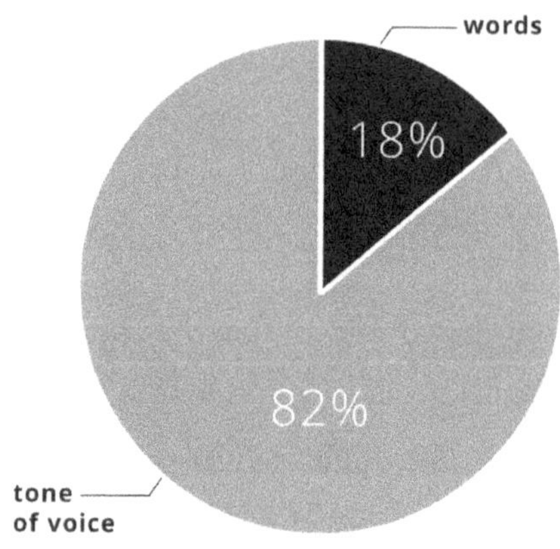

But how do most people communicate at work? It's not face-to-face! No, most work communication takes place over email—and also Slack, MS Teams, Google Chat, or whatever messaging app your company uses.

When we rely on digital communication, we completely lose the ability to interpret body language and vocal tone, which is what our brains crave for clarity. This is highly problematic and leads to misinterpretations, miscommunications—and, far too often, assumptions and judgments. This is especially true if people's communication styles are dissimilar (we'll get to that in a minute).

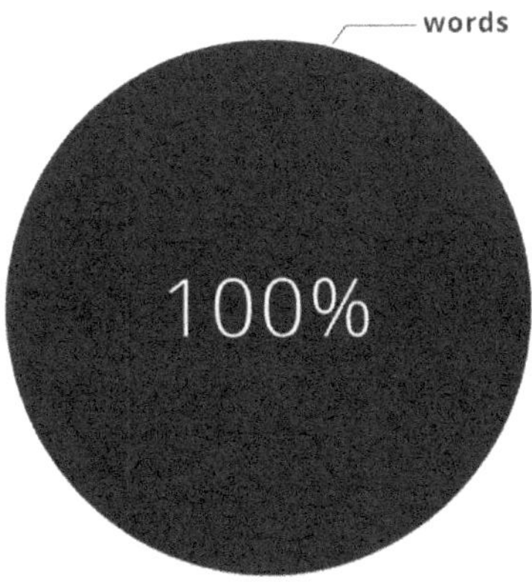

The golden rule of digital communication is: *Words are never read in the tone of the sender. They are always interpreted through the recipient's lens of insecurity.* This is especially true if you, a leader, are sending emails to people who report to you. There is a power dynamic that you must consider when sending emails, especially if you are a one-line emailer.

To effectively communicate via email, you need to ensure that you've included tone and intent that meets the communication needs of your audience. If you send an email or message that simply states, "Please come see me in my office," you risk a potential freakout on the other side of that message. Emails like that create emotional stress—which does what?

Yup, it triggers the amygdala and puts the recipient in a fear response. By the time they get to your office, they're in full-on fight or flight mode. This is not productive. The kicker is, you may have written that email in a neutral or even a giddy mood. Maybe you have good news to share. Maybe you're about to offer them a promotion. Maybe you have cupcakes for them, or even Metallica tickets! No matter what your intent, I can guarantee you that most people who read "see me in my office" will immediately think, "I'm losing my job today."

I'm not suggesting that you stop using email. That would be silly. Digital communication allows us to communicate important info to a broad audience immediately. How handy! But sometimes, email is used for conversations that should never, ever be digital. Redirection conversations, disciplinary conversations, layoff notices, and reorganization conversations are best had in person so tone and body language are on full display. If that isn't feasible, hold them via video chat, or at least on the phone.

The second thing to consider is the way you word the info you're delivering. This can be challenging on a few levels, but it will make sense as you reframe why you're communicating in the first place.

Remember, your job as a leader is to motivate and coach your teams. Shifting your language to generative speech will prevent an accidental amygdala trigger. I call this method of redirection *humble structure.*

Many times, when we explain a procedure or a request to someone, we end with, "Do you understand?" or "Does that make sense to you?" Those words seem innocuous enough, but the onus in those questions is on the person being trained.

Now, this may sound silly, but a lot of folks, especially folks who see you in a position of power, don't want to appear stupid or be a burden, so they will just say, "Yup!" and think to themselves, *I'll figure it out later.* This does not bode well for efficiency, learning, and trust-building.

Instead, you could end your teaching session with something like, "Did I explain that well?" or "I'm not sure if I conveyed that well, so you probably have questions." Now the onus is on you and takes the pressure off the learner. They'll be more amenable to asking their questions because you have normalized it. If you're thinking, *But I do explain things well and they just don't get it*, your ego has gotten the best of you. Egocentric management leads to Funked-up Boss Syndrome.

Think about it. You're training a new person. Using the humble structure strategy, you mention that maybe you didn't explain it really well and ask how you could do better. The new person is like, "Whew, this is a human who cares and is willing to help me understand." Now you've allowed trust to build, you're learning more about this new person and how they learn, and at the end of the whole thing, they will *actually learn* the thing you need them to know instead of just faking it till they make it. You've led them beautifully in that moment. Ego not necessary. And honestly, no one is going to be like, "Ugh. My boss is so helpful. What a weakling!" (Which is what your ego is scared of.)

The second thing to consider is communication behavior. Are you reacting or responding? Reaction is an emotional brain response from the Hot Zone, whereas response comes from the Cool Zone and a place of emotional intelligence—and you know now which Zone you want to lead from.

And then, there's the missing piece to the puzzle: communication styles. Not everyone learns and communicates the same way. If the person in front of you doesn't share your communication style, it's actually possible that you didn't explain the procedure well enough *for them.*

SPOCK OR KIRK? COMMUNICATION STYLES

The various preferences and styles we demonstrate when we're communicating add another layer of complexity to the communication conundrum.

Over the course of my career, I have used numerous popular assessment tools including DISC, the Enneagram, and CliftonStrengths (formerly StrengthsFinder) when working with companies, leaders, and teams. I have a ton of respect for all of those systems, but over time I realized that we need to look at the combination of all three, plus some other factors, in order to truly change the way we communicate with and understand others.

To this end, I created the Communication Compass, which provides guidance and direction related to each of five core communication styles, and explores how their outward expression is based on their internal drivers, desires, needs, and fears.

The five Communication Compass styles are:

- Assertive
- Logical
- Supportive
- Inspiring
- Collaborative

THE COMMUNICATION COMPASS

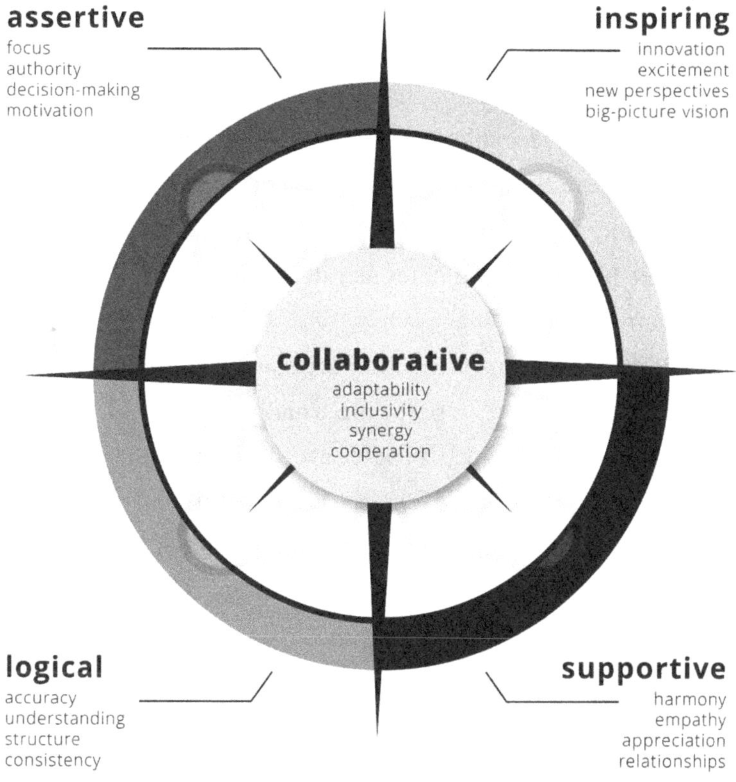

To find your Communication Compass style, start by checking out the illustration above and the descriptions on the following pages to see what fits you best. (Or, even better, go to **www.unfunkyourselfbook.com** to take the full Communication Compass assessment for free!)

There is no "right" style for leaders. There is no "good" or "bad" style. Each has its own unique strengths and challenges.

Nor are there any absolutes. How we communicate is an adapted, fluid state based on our environment, situation, expectations, and the other people involved. Your default style today may be different than it was ten years ago, and also different from how it will be five years from now.

Once you've explored the five styles, you may see that you are intensely dominant in one area. Or, you may have a tie or almost-tie of two or more styles. All of these results are completely normal and demonstrate the complexity of human communication.

Assertive and Inspiring folks are usually extroverted, while Logical and Supportive peeps are usually introverted. Further, Assertive and Logical people are task-oriented, whereas Inspiring and Supportive folks are relationship-oriented. Those differences alone can cause confusion and conflict because we're not on the same page with each other.

The Collaborators are chameleon-esque, easily shifting through approaches depending on the demands of the conversation, situation, and audience. They are in some ways a combination of all of the other styles (which is why you'll see them in the center of the Communication Compass), but they also have their own very precise needs and drivers.

Let's explore the five Communication Compass styles. In each section below, I'll break out the interaction style, desires, needs, and fears of each style. I'll also share each style's misinterpretations (how other people misperceive its motivations and actions) and also its clarification (meaning, what it truly represents and seeks to accomplish).

ASSERTIVE

Interaction

Extrovert

Desires

- *Control.* To take charge of situations and influence outcomes.
- *Achievement.* To set and accomplish ambitious goals.
- *Respect.* To be seen as competent and authoritative.

Needs

- *Clarity.* Clear expectations and objectives.
- *Autonomy.* Freedom to make decisions and act independently.
- *Feedback.* Direct, honest feedback on performance and results.

Fears

- *Loss of Control.* Fearing situations where they cannot influence outcomes or decisions.
- *Failure.* Concern over not meeting their own or others' expectations for success.
- *Being Undermined.* Worrying that their authority will be challenged or disrespected.

Misinterpretation

Seen as bossy, impatient, or insensitive to others' ideas and emotions, the Assertive communicator's directness and focus on action can come across as domineering, especially to those who value collaboration or reflection. Others might feel they're pushing their agenda without considering different viewpoints.

Clarification

Assertive communicators are typically highly committed to achieving goals and ensuring the team succeeds. They value decisiveness and often believe that taking charge helps everyone stay on track.

LOGICAL

Interaction

Introvert

Desires

- *Understanding.* To gain insight and knowledge through analysis.
- *Accuracy.* To ensure that details are correct and that information is reliable.
- *Structure.* To work within well-defined systems and processes.

Needs

- *Information.* Access to data, facts, and thorough explanations.

- *Time.* Sufficient time to think, process, and respond.
- *Consistency.* A stable environment where procedures are followed.

Fears

- *Incompetence.* Fear of being perceived as unknowledgeable or incorrect.
- *Chaos.* Discomfort with environments that lack structure or clear guidelines.
- *Overwhelm.* Anxiety about being overloaded with information or tasks without adequate support.

Misinterpretation

Perceived as detached, overly critical, or unapproachable, Logical communicators prioritize facts, data, and logic over emotions, which can sometimes make them seem cold or dismissive. Their tendency to focus on details and question assumptions may be taken as a lack of trust or resistance to new ideas.

Clarification

Analytical communicators simply want to ensure accuracy and make well-informed decisions. They aim to be thorough and objective, not dismissive or resistant, and they value clear thinking and reliability.

SUPPORTIVE

Interaction

Introvert

Desires

- *Connection.* To build meaningful relationships with others.
- *Harmony.* To maintain a peaceful and supportive environment.
- *Appreciation.* To feel valued and recognized for their contributions.

Needs

- *Empathy.* Understanding and compassion from others.
- *Collaboration.* Opportunities to work with others in a supportive manner.
- *Reassurance.* Positive feedback that validates their efforts and intentions.

Fears

- *Rejection.* Fear of not being accepted or valued by others.
- *Conflict.* Anxiety about disharmony in relationships or team dynamics.
- *Invisibility.* Worry that their contributions will go unnoticed or unappreciated.

Misinterpretation

Viewed as overly accommodating, hesitant, or lacking assertiveness, the Supportive communicator's focus on harmony and empathy can be mistaken for a lack of confidence or inability to make tough decisions. Others might see them as prioritizing relationships over results, especially in high-stakes situations.

Clarification

Supportive communicators are genuinely concerned about team cohesion and individual well-being. They often serve as the emotional glue in groups, working to ensure that everyone feels valued and heard, which they see as essential for long-term success.

INSPIRING

Interaction

Extrovert

Desires

- *Excitement.* To engage in lively, stimulating conversations and experiences.
- *Variety.* To explore new ideas and creative solutions.
- *Recognition.* To be acknowledged for their creativity and enthusiasm.

Needs

- *Freedom.* The ability to express ideas without constraints.

- *Positivity.* An encouraging environment that fosters optimism and enthusiasm.
- *Interaction.* Opportunities for dynamic interaction and brainstorming with others.

Fears

- *Boredom.* Fear of routine and stagnation that stifles creativity and enthusiasm.
- *Being Limited.* Concern over restrictions that inhibit their ability to express ideas freely.
- *Disappointment.* Worry that their ideas or visions will be rejected or dismissed by others.

Misinterpretation

Inspiring communicators bring energy and enthusiasm, often thinking creatively and spontaneously, but may be seen as impractical, inconsistent, or distracted. Others may view their abundance of ideas as scattered or overly optimistic, especially if the ideas seem ungrounded in reality.

Clarification

Inspiring communicators are passionate about innovation and new perspectives. They strive to bring fresh thinking to the team, hoping to energize others and foster a dynamic, open environment. Their big-picture thinking is meant to inspire, not to detract from practical goals.

COLLABORATIVE

Interaction

Ambivert

Desires

- *Inclusion.* To ensure everyone's voice is heard and valued.
- *Synergy.* To create solutions that combine multiple perspectives for innovation.
- *Cooperation.* To foster teamwork and collective problem-solving.

Needs

- *Open Dialogue.* Opportunities for honest communication and feedback from all team members.
- *Diverse Perspectives.* Exposure to different ideas and viewpoints to enrich discussions.
- *Shared Goals.* Clear, common objectives that unify team efforts and promote collaboration.

Fears

- *Exclusion.* Fear of not being included in conversations or decision-making processes.
- *Conflict Among Team Members.* Anxiety about disharmony that could disrupt collaboration and teamwork.

- *Failure to Integrate.* Concern that differing viewpoints will lead to divisiveness rather than constructive outcomes.

Misinterpretation
Collaborative communicators aim to include everyone's perspectives, and can therefore be perceived as indecisive, overly focused on consensus, or lacking individual conviction. Others may misinterpret their preference for integration as a lack of independent thought, and see them as slowing down decision-making or avoiding difficult choices.

Clarification
Collaborative communicators believe that everyone has valuable input and that the best solutions come from considering diverse viewpoints. They are driven by a desire for unity and believe that integrated decisions lead to more sustainable and inclusive outcomes.

***

Demonstrating how the various styles express and communicate in live workshops is interactive and illustrative, but in a book, it can be a bit dry. To liven things up, I'll analyze some well-known and well-loved characters.

Let's get nerdy!

The Star Trek Communication Compass (Original and Aughts Movies)

Kirk (Assertive)

Confident and action-oriented, Kirk is known for taking charge, especially in critical situations, and wooing all the alien ladies. He has a strong drive to lead his crew toward success. He's decisive, sometimes even bold, but values the loyalty of his team and often places the mission above all else. His key desire is achievement and control over outcomes. His primary fear is failure or loss of control. Kirk's willingness to take risks and make quick decisions in the face of danger showcases his strong leadership style. His assertiveness often inspires his team to act courageously under pressure.

Spock (Logical)

Methodical, rational, and detail-oriented, Spock embodies the analytical communicator, valuing facts, logic, and clear thinking. He is often the voice of reason on the bridge, providing insights grounded in data and logic. His key desire is accuracy and understanding, whereas his primary fear is incompetence or emotional interference with rational decisions. Spock's logical approach to problem-solving helps the crew navigate complex situations, especially when emotions run high. His analytical mind ensures that decisions are based on the most accurate information available. No other style is logical, Captain.

Dr. Leonard "Bones" McCoy (Supportive)

Though he claps back with a bit of snark—"Dammit Jim, I'm a doctor, not a mechanic!"—Dr. McCoy is a compassionate, loyal, and emotionally intelligent team "connector," often providing emotional support and understanding to other crew members. He values harmony and is unafraid to speak up for his friends, showing deep empathy. His key desire is connection and harmony, whereas his primary fear is rejection or conflict within the crew. McCoy's support for Kirk and Spock creates a sense of balance on the team, especially when he reminds them of the human cost of their actions. His warmth and concern for others make him a grounding presence on the Enterprise.

Scotty (Inspiring)

Energetic, inventive, and resourceful, Scotty, the Chief Engineer, is enthusiastic and endlessly creative, often finding innovative solutions to keep the Enterprise running under challenging conditions. He thrives in situations that allow him to think outside the box. His key desire is excitement and recognition for his ingenuity, whereas his primary fear is boredom or being constrained by limits. Scotty's creative solutions and love for his work are evident every time he pulls off an engineering miracle to save the crew. His passion for engineering keeps the team's morale high, and his enthusiasm often inspires others, even when there is danger afoot: "Aye, the haggis is in the fire now for sure."

Uhura (Collaborative)

Diplomatic, adaptable, and inclusive, Uhura exemplifies the collaborative communicator by integrating perspectives and facilitating communication. As the Communications Officer, she ensures smooth interactions, both within the crew and with alien species, emphasizing inclusivity and teamwork. Her key desires are inclusion and cooperation, whereas her primary fear is exclusion or discord within the team. Uhura's role often involves bridging gaps and managing conflicts, whether that's translating alien languages or mediating difficult conversations. Her ability to see and appreciate multiple perspectives helps unify the crew, highlighting the importance of collaboration. She excels at bringing everyone to the proverbial table for negotiation and solutions. "Hailing frequencies are open, Captain!"

Applying the Communication Compass to Non-Fantasy Workplaces

Why does all of this matter, you ask? Because although we are all similar to one another, our tendencies and responses to stimuli are different. This becomes apparent when we are working in teams or faced with stressful decisions.

One of the funniest moments I've experienced in my career happened during a Mindful Leader Practice workshop training that I facilitated with a group from a state's department of transportation. During the Communication Compass activity, participants respond to a theoretical situation using their default style's approach. Then, we spend time comparing the approaches and looking at the similarities and differences (okay, mostly the differences).

This activity illuminates the different communication approaches that so often lead to misunderstandings, miscommunication, and for some, hurt feelings. For example, someone who is an Assertive style (direct, goal-oriented, and fast-paced) may deliver information to a Supportive style (indirect, gentle, relationship-oriented, and slower-paced) in a manner that appears to be rude or insensitive. The Assertive style doesn't mean to be rude; they're just mindlessly approaching communication in their default style. I then ask people to approach the activity from the style that least represents them so that we can uncover the assumptions they make about that style and the behaviors that follow. It's a fascinating activity and often highly amusing.

In this particular workshop, it became apparent that there was serious tension between some members of upper management and their mid-line managers. There were allusions to upper management bullying, not caring, and generally being funked up.

Toward the end of the activity, a voice boomed from the corner of the room, "Holy shit, Chuck. You're not an asshole. You're just an Assertive!"

After a beat of stunned silence, the entire room broke out in genuine laughter. This light-bulb moment was followed by many others in which people who'd been working together for years finally gained insight into the communication styles of their colleagues. All sorts of ASJs, annoyances, misunderstandings, and hurt feelings were illuminated and alleviated that day.

Interpersonal communication is more about *how* you communicate than *what* you communicate. Done well, it ensures your audience captures the information the way you need them to. If you communicate in a way that makes someone uncomfortable, guess what? Their amygdala fires and they jump ship from their analytical brain to their emotional brain. So, if you've ever wrapped up a big presentation, looked around the room, and thought, "They just don't get it," you're sort of right. They may *not* get it, and they may even be getting all Hot Zone about it, because you did not meet their needs and deliver in a way that was accessible to their communication style.

It's okay. It happens to everyone. But now that you're practicing mindfulness, you will start to notice that the eyes of the Assertive and Inspiring types glaze over when you share too many details, the Logicals glance around in confusion when you talk all big-picture and no process, and the Supportives want to know *why* it all matters and how it will affect people's experiences. The Collaboratives would really like everyone on the same page, please, so we can make some decisions?

Knowing your own style is the first step in communicating well. The second (and just as important) step is figuring out the styles and subsequent needs of the folks who work with and for you. Determining how to deliver information to your audience's various styles is a key ingredient of un-funked leadership.

For example, I'm typically an Assertive-Inspiring, which means when I'm presenting I need to slow down and explain the "why" and "how" as well as the "what" so all styles can get on board. However, when I have a chance to analyze the social psychology of any group, even fictitious ones, my Logical tendencies come roaring to the forefront coupled with my default Inspiring tendencies to blab to anyone who will listen. (Or read. Aren't you lucky?) Knowing this, I have learned to take a step back and practice social awareness when I go into super-nerd mode so I don't totally turn off my coworkers, family, or random strangers in the airport.

When you're communicating individually, you can tailor your approach to make sure it's received by the person in front of you. To meet the needs of a group, you'll need to speak to all styles. The simplest way to do this is present as a Collaborative:

start with the big-picture vision or concept for each topic along with the bottom line and then add in the details and the emotional "why" to elaborate. This approach allows the Assertive and Inspiring styles to make quick decisions right away and gives the Logical and Supportive styles an opportunity to methodically determine the key steps in the process.

So, have you connected the dots between recent interactions and your own communication style? What about your reports? Your boss? The team member who appears to be afraid of you? Can you spot where some miscommunications might be occurring between you and your team members? How can you better approach communication with them?

Even if you think you know your style based on what you just read, please go to **www.unfunkyourselfbook.com** to take the Communication Compass assessment so you can start approaching all of your conversations more mindfully. If you want to go big, request a Mindful Leader Practice workshop from me (shameless plug) so you and your teams can start using the Communication Compass in real time together.

OTHER CONSIDERATIONS REGARDING COMMUNICATION

Adding even more complexity to the communication conundrum are cultural differences and neurodiversities. I learned this in a most uncomfortable way when volunteering for a refugee resettlement program in New England.

A colleague and I, along with an interpreter, were working with a young couple relocating to the U.S. from Afghanistan. As we went through the intake process, asking questions and gathering information, the wife seemed like she wasn't actively engaged. Her eyes were trained on the floor, and her husband was becoming more and more agitated.

Around the fourth question, the husband made an angry remark, stood up, and walked out of the room. I asked the interpreter what was going on and was informed that in Afghan culture, it is inappropriate for a woman to make and hold eye contact with a man to whom she isn't related or married.

I, of course, had been making direct eye contact with this gentleman for the entire intake session, and also attempting to do so with his wife, because in American culture eye contact signals attentiveness, care, and active listening.

Think what you will about that particular cultural dynamic, but my attempt at engaging via eye contact was an amygdala-triggering action for this couple that threatened the conversation and the entire purpose of the meeting. The goal was for me to gather information, because my job was to get this family situated as quickly and safely as possible. Therefore, I needed to be aware of and sensitive to the cultural nuances of the people I was trying to help.

For a split second, my brain (and tripped amygdala) sarcastically said, "*Pfft.* Welcome to America. Might as well get used to eyeballs looking at you." But I quickly shifted into an empathetic space when I remembered that, not only had these folks fled their native land to the safety of the U.S., enduring intense pain and fear in that transition alone, but also the person they were banking on to help them (me) was violating all sorts of cultural boundaries. I asked the interpreter to apologize to the couple for me and ask if they would be okay if we resumed the process and I would avert my gaze. They agreed, and I spent the remainder of the interview looking just at the screen into which I was typing their info. It was *so* uncomfortable for me—especially since I could no longer rely on the visual and nonverbal cues that, remember, make up more than 77 percent of human communication—but it was necessary to shift my communication style to get the job done and get this couple into their new home.

I've relayed this story a few times in workshops and to colleagues. One of the most common questions is, "Did your behavior constitute a 'fawning' response?"

What a great question. The answer is no.

Although my amygdala was slightly triggered, as evidenced by my inner sarcasm, I was not experiencing fear in that moment, so my shift wasn't fawning. I wasn't placating a perceived abuser or attempting to diffuse a violent situation. Rather, I was adjusting my approach to meet the communication and culture needs of a frightened and vulnerable couple who had just crossed an ocean with nothing but a few suitcases—and who were kind enough to forgive my mistake once they realized our misunderstanding.

I am writing this book from an American perspective. Other cultures approach communication, including various nonverbal cues, quite differently than Americans do. And while most American communication strategies probably won't be fatal in boardrooms in Europe, Australia, Central America, or South America, take them to China, Japan, India, or the Middle East (to name a few places), and you run the risk of accidentally derailing the conversation before it even begins.

As a leader, it's important to understand that there will be differences in how folks from other cultures approach communication. Do what I didn't do before sitting down with that Afghani couple: your research. If you don't know—or you don't know what you don't know—just ask. Most people are happy and even excited to inform you about proper communication etiquette in their culture.

Consider as well the reality of different neurotypes we encounter daily. I've become incredibly familiar with various neurotypes in the last few years, and I realize that the neurotype landscape is broad to say the least. I would argue that every single one of us is on some sort of spectrum of some sort of neurotype. Our brains, and the ways in which they work, are not identical.

Having said that, there are some neurotypes that have much bigger tells: ADHD, dyslexia, anxiety, OCD, and the whole constellation of profiles in the autism spectrum disorder (ASD) realm.

I refuse to refer to the above as "mental illnesses" because they are not diseases. They are neurotypes—brain wiring patterns—and although perhaps different from what you might be used to encountering, they are not weird, incompetent, or stupid.

A former colleague, a proudly autistic person, once explained to me that full-on eye contact feels really intense for him and spikes his anxiety. When that happens, he can't think straight (hello, amygdala, you silly beast!). So, he prefers to look at his notebook and take notes when working with other people instead of engaging directly. Another colleague needs to fidget or walk around in meetings due to her ADHD; moving helps her process information and also calms her nervous system which is constantly seeking stimulation.

Your job as a human is to know your own brain, your neurotype, your culture, and what those things mean to and for you. Your job as a leader is to acknowledge and honor that everyone, everywhere has some neurospice happening, and probably has cultural nuances as well. You just have to be open-minded and see past your definitions and "shoulds" into a broader sense of human community.

Have you ever experienced someone violating your cultural norms or invalidating your neurotype? Or, maybe you've found yourself in the same spot I was in, unknowingly upsetting someone by violating their cultural communication norms. What social awareness cues did you learn from those experiences?

UN-FUNK YOUR COMMUNICATION

Think about your colleagues or the folks on your team.

- Who, does it seem, just "doesn't get it"?
- Who, in your estimation, is rude?
- Who, perhaps, is "too emotional"?
- What about the team member who is only about the facts and doesn't want to chit-chat with you ... do you think they are aloof?
- After reading this chapter, where do you think you might be experiencing a mismatch in communication styles?

Ask your team members to read through the Communication Compass style descriptions in this chapter and discuss their styles. Use this as a team-building opportunity as well as a chance get to know your employees better. You can also grab a handy tool to support your team on the book resources page at **www.unfunkyourselfbook.com**.

CHAPTER EIGHT

CONFLICT NAVIGATION

XAVIER, A CISO for a mid-sized financial institution, was experiencing constant conflict with other members of the C-suite.

"They don't care about information security," he explained. "They say, 'There are complaints about the restrictions that the infosec team implemented. They're not convenient for the employees.' But those restrictions are in place to prevent security breaches and make sure bad actors don't compromise customer data. Not to mention protecting the company from lawsuits."

He was really upset that the security policies were not just being treated lightly, but often blatantly ignored. Some requirements were being circumvented by both employees and managers.

Bradley, Xavier's boss, addressed the policy violations in a way that was performative at best. "Employees shouldn't do these things," he told Xavier, "but the business needs to be successful, and it will be fine."

"It would be less painful to slam my head into a wall," Xavier groaned. "If we're ever breached, it's my neck on the line, not theirs."

It probably won't surprise you to learn that morale was low in this company, and that finger-pointing and blame-shifting were commonplace within the leadership team.

The swirling conflict was no one person's fault. It was the fault of several funked-up bosses who were misaligned and who miscommunicated as a rule.

Xavier's focus was on keeping data and customer information safe. Bradley's focus was on keeping the business humming and making money. When we added in the other C-level folks and what they were personally focused on, we ended up with a group of siloed thinkers—each in their own bubble, seeing their own department's needs as primary and everyone else's as peripheral.

Xavier, Bradley, and the other C-levels were in perpetual conflict, but they weren't really disagreeing about anything. They couldn't get as far as actual disagreement because they weren't on the same page. None of them had a full understanding of the others' issues, requests, and resource needs. None had taken the time to pause, consider that they might not know everything that was going on, and ask questions to understand context and needs. Instead, each of them fell prey to rampant ASJs, and then became frustrated and irritated based on those "truths."

After I facilitated intense communication work and deep organizational concept mapping, the group realized that they needed to actively listen to each other rather than trying to force the others to hear them. Listening to learn, rather than listening to respond, is how each is beginning to appreciate the full what, why, and how of the organization's overall needs. Once this more mindful level of communication was in play, it's my hope and intention that it will be simple for Xavier and Bradley to design a protocol that is both user-friendly and compliant with the organization's security needs.

HOW DO YOU HANDLE CONFLICT?

The word conflict, derived from the Latin word *conflictus*, literally translates as "to strike together; to fight, to struggle." Not the most pleasant idea.

When I ask audiences to give me some words that correlate with "conflict," I usually hear words like *disagreement*, *argument*, *anger*, *miscommunication*, *misalignment*—and once, "Obnoxious asshole!"

Alrighty then.

Of course, there is always one person in my workshops who emphatically adds, "Opportunity to learn!"

I don't disagree with that, as being mindful will always allow us to see opportunities in our challenges, but I follow up by asking, "Is that a real-life thought or a wish list thought? Do you *actually* see conflict as an opportunity, or is it a massive, time-wasting pain in the ass that sometimes has a learning curve attached?"

The knowing laughter that follows gives the real answer away.

Most people aren't comfortable in conflictual situations—which makes sense since, as we've covered, conflict creates emotional stress (and sometimes physical threat), which triggers the amygdala, which sends us into fight/flight/freeze/fawn mode where we swirl around in our emotional brain. Not fun. That's why most people prefer to avoid conflict altogether, rather than entertain that discomfort in the short term—even if they know that addressing it will have long-term benefits.

What conflict avoiders often don't realize is that conflictual situations don't just go away on their own. In fact, it's quite the opposite; they often fester, creating more and bigger problems and therefore more and bigger conflicts. The "ostrich method" of conflict management does not work, and it's especially detrimental for leaders.

So, what if I told you that conflict doesn't have to be negative, painful, or hard? And, what if I told you that the discomfort of conflict has more to do with you than with the situation itself, and that you can minimize it by expanding your self-awareness and self-management?

It all comes back to being mindful and knowing your identity, ASJs, and triggers. To quote the fictional, yet fascinating, Captain Jack Sparrow, "The problem is not the problem. The problem is your attitude about the problem."

Remember Jeff from Chapter Two? The guy who wanted his entire team to log on to Zoom for the eight-hour workday? Well, the problem wasn't that everyone had to work from home. The problem was his *discomfort, fear, insecurity, assumptions,* and *judgments* about everyone working from home, coupled with all the other uncontrollable things about a global pandemic. This discomfort led him to create a much bigger issue than was necessary. Squarely in his emotional brain, he turned an uncomfortable yet manageable situation into, as my BFF Heidi would say, "a total goat rodeo." Not as destructive as a dumpster fire, but still chaotic, frustrating, and a bit out of control.

His fear of the unknown—"OMG, what the hell is COVID-19?"—combined with conforming to a government-imposed lockdown over which he had no control, not being in his "happy place" (the office), not being in the physical vicinity of his team, and not trusting his ability to manage a team remotely was a recipe for disastrous internal conflict that became external as he attempted to assert control. What could have been an awkward but generally positive pivot for the team became a goat rodeo that cost him time, money, trust, respect, and ultimately, his job.

Conflict stems from all sorts of places, many of which we cannot control. That said, we can and should control our *reactions* to conflictual situations. Lack of control in itself is a conflict catalyst. Mindful human beings crave autonomy and control over themselves so they can respond appropriately when shit happens. Mindless humans crave control over others. (More on that later.)

Let's explore some of the most common roots of workplace conflict. All of these, as you're about to learn, can be minimized or totally resolved when a mindful leadership approach is applied.

MISALIGNMENT

Alignment is when everyone involved in a project, situation, or team dynamic understands exactly what their role is and what is expected of them. Facilitating alignment is an act of mindfulness and respect. Your job as a leader is to ensure everyone has exactly what they need to go forth and do The Thing really well, feel good about themselves and their work, and remain motivated. This includes setting expectations and creating accountability, but also applying emotional intelligence to ensure everyone feels heard, seen, and supported.

Misalignment arises when people don't understand what is expected of them, don't have the information or resources they need to do The Thing, or don't feel supported and acknowledged by leadership. Misalignment, and the communication missteps it creates, is one of the biggest sources of workplace conflict and the number one way in which team members feel their bosses are funked up.

When you create alignment, you can focus on your stuff without worrying about their stuff. Simple, right? Well, yes … and no. You see, alignment requires clarity, and clarity can only come from a full understanding of your audience's skills and abilities, communication style and needs, and level of comfort with your direction. In other words, mindfulness creates alignment.

To ensure you and your team are on the same page, you must set expectations in a way that meets their comprehension needs. This goes back to knowing your own and their communication styles and identifying the areas where you need to lean into their needs.

So, when you lay out a plan, instead of assuming everyone's got it, ask them to repeat back to you what the plan is, explaining that you want to ensure that you communicated it well. Remember to employ humble structure in these moments. When the onus of delivering well is on you, others are more likely to ask for clarification and help. By asking them to explain the plan back to you, you'll determine both their actual level of understanding and the level of mindfulness and skill of your own communication.

LOW EMOTIONAL INTELLIGENCE

I know we've covered this already, but it's so incredibly important that I'm adding it here again. Lack of self-awareness and lack of empathy will render all of your other leadership skills and strategies useless. When you know yourself and practice mindfulness, you can manage your own emotions, which means you can also effectively communicate with and connect to your team. Trust requires connection, and leadership requires trust.

Mindful leaders possess high emotional intelligence and practice mindful pauses so they can respond logically rather than react emotionally. Bad Bosses react from their own fears, traumas, identities, and ASJs, and then wonder why the heck everyone is scared of and frustrated by them.

Please, please, *please* go back to Chapter Six and take the time to work through your self-awareness and social awareness if you haven't already done so. It can feel like a grind at first, but the benefits are immeasurable, especially once you master shifting from a reactive emotional state to a responsive one.

MISCOMMUNICATION

We discussed how communication style differences must be considered when issuing directives, redirection, and setting expectations.

Mindlessly communicating from your default style without considering the style(s) of your intended audience can lead to confusion, misunderstandings, and frustration for everyone involved. For example, as an Assertive/Inspiring style, I tend to speak in big-picture language, painting a vision and an idea with a timeline. However, when pressed for details about how to make the vision a reality, my usual response is, "We'll figure it out." For my Logical and Supportive colleagues, this is beyond annoying, and also unnerving, as these folks require details, data, examples, and compelling reasons to feel confident and comfortable executing a plan. I cannot expect my Logical and Supportive colleagues to buy into my vision if I haven't defined the idea to meet their needs and they don't have a process to follow. It's unfair, disrespectful, and counterproductive.

Similarly, Logical and Supportive leaders tend to frustrate Assertive and Inspiring team members because they often skip the big picture in favor of the details and process. Assertive styles will always ask, "What's the end game," or "What's the bottom line?" while Inspiring peeps want to know, "Why should I buy in? What's the vision?"

Communication also includes listening. *Active* listening.

Stephen Covey famously observed that, "Most people do not listen with the intent to understand. They listen with the intent to reply. They're either speaking or preparing to speak. They're filtering everything through their own paradigms, reading their autobiography into other people's lives."

Often, when someone is explaining their point of view to us, especially in a debate or disagreement, our amygdala dimmer switch is ticking up, and our ASJs are armed and ready to shoot down any point the other person makes. We're not listening or looking for places where our beliefs or identities overlap. We're looking for weak spots to aim for so we can win the "fight."

Active listening is the Green Zone in action. It's curiosity in motion. It's pausing to hear, understand, and absorb the information that someone is telling you *even if you disagree with them.*

Active listening also requires that you demonstrate that you hear what they are saying by acknowledging the information you're receiving, including asking clarifying questions to make sure you're on the same page.

SKILLS/ABILITIES GAP

I once had to learn a notoriously difficult graphic design program for a project. My boss said, "Oh, it's super easy. You'll figure it out," and assigned the project to me with no further information or support.

I Googled and YouTubed like my life depended on it, but after a few days of futzing with the software and getting nowhere, I approached my boss for help. She was a bit miffed that I wasn't further along, and the due date was looming. I asked her to just walk me through how to use the software, to which she responded, "If I'm going to do that, I might as well do the thing myself."

After a short debate about the accuracy of that statement, it became evident that she didn't know how to use the software either.

I was a wee bit pissed off because she'd made it my issue and was starting to blame me for the lack of results when she'd basically set me an impossible task. I definitely approached assignments from her with more caution from that point forward, which led her to observe that I was "hedging" rather than committing to projects. Well, of course I was. I was going in blind!

Most of us can recall at least one situation where we were totally flying by the seat of our pants, with pretty much zero idea what we were doing. You might be in such a situation right now. Sometimes, expectations are heaped on us, and we just have to figure it out. This is where conflict can happen.

Learning new stuff is cool, and we should all aspire to learn and grow. But when you're on a deadline and you don't have the skills to fulfill the demand, what could have been a fun challenge turns into an amygdala-triggering stress-fest.

As a rule, it's never a good idea to assign something new to someone if you can't provide resources to help them learn. You don't have to know how to do The Thing, but you do need to know how to help someone learn it. If you can't do that, you'll need to source someone who does.

LACK OF RESOURCES

Budget cuts, reorganizations, and layoffs are a major part of the leadership gauntlet. In some cases, you as a leader don't have control over these major decisions—and even if you do, there's often a board of directors calling the shots.

Cuts, reorgs, and layoffs always result in one challenging reality for those remaining: fewer people who need to do more work on a smaller budget. Some companies, like the mortgage lender for whom my friend Gordon works, also ask employees to take a pay cut and forego bonuses and raises, as well as manage extra work. Gordon hasn't seen a raise in four years, yet his workload has increased by at least 30 percent.

Efficiency is one thing, but asking people who are already performing at capacity to do more with less is a ridiculous request. You know it as well as I do. And no matter how leaders try to spin it, people feel betrayed, undervalued, overworked, and underpaid. In fact, I would argue that the responsibility for today's "quiet quitting" movement rests squarely on leadership who are attempting to squeeze blood from proverbial stones. Want to know why all your employees are burned out? Look no further.

Morale is fragile even in the best companies. Good times create high morale, but the minute there is a tremor in the foundation—executive leadership changes, budget cuts, layoffs—that scale tips quickly. Attrition in these times is a given.

The advice I provide to clients when layoffs or reorgs are unavoidable is simply to be transparent and prepare for the fallout. Remember, humans don't like ambiguity and will seek clarification to allay their fear and discomfort. If they don't receive clarification, they will create the answers in their heads and run with them as truth. They will then share their various theories with others in an attempt to build alliances and protect their own interests (tribe mentality). It makes us feel better to have connections and friends, especially in tough times.

LACK OF TRANSPARENCY

Speaking of transparency ...

Employees are not stupid, nor are they islands unto themselves. They talk to each other, and when there's ambiguity, they will create the answers (see above). This kind of assumption leads to drama, drama leads to culture mayhem, mayhem leads to attrition, and attrition leads to even bigger drama and morale issues. You can contain the conflict from the outset.

For example, a client of mine, a software-as-a-service (SaaS) company, banked on a 10 percent attrition rate during a barely explained and poorly timed layoff session. The idea was that 10 percent of the employee base would leave on their own after the layoffs happened, but since they weren't laid off, the company wouldn't have to provide severance. They also had no plans to backfill these spots; the attrition was part of their strategy to decrease expenses.

This is a fairly common practice. It's also super shady and guaranteed to cause conflict within your workforce.

Due to the lack of transparency around the layoffs as well as the poor timing, the client instead experienced an abrupt 30 percent staff loss which included 70 percent of their product development department. They were left flailing and poised to fail in the marketplace.

I was brought on after the mass exodus, which also included scathing reviews on Glassdoor.com that impacted the company's ability to hire people to fill the vacant roles. My job was to help "fix morale" and help with recruitment/retention efforts.

Admittedly, I was hesitant to work with this group—not because I couldn't do the job, but because their expectations were unrealistic. You can't just "fix" morale. It's not a broken lamp that you just Superglue back together and hide the seams. It's a long and complex process which requires, at the very least, humility, honesty, transparency, and dialogue from everyone as trust and confidence are rebuilt and amygdala dimmer switches are gradually dialed down. I am very good at what I do, but I cannot counteract years of Funked-Up Boss behavior in a few weeks! Quick-fix thinking like this is what led this company into their particular goat rodeo in the first place.

The executive leadership team deemed this an employee issue. I argued that all of this actually stemmed from Funked-Up Bossery—from them, in general, and from their risky gamble specifically. After all, the gamble itself came on the heels of years of stagnant pay, multiple internal reorganizations, numerous product changes, layered work, minimal resources, and general emotional malaise.

The leadership group discovered that they were woefully disconnected from their staff and that, in their drive to be successful and innovative, they had never considered the needs and concerns of the humans tasked with process implementation and repeated product changes.

After many months of whole-company team-building work, organizational effectiveness planning, and the resignation of the COO (who, thankfully, took his company-over-people attitude with him), employee satisfaction began to rise. Productivity increased, and employees began to make referrals for open positions. Today, product-related decisions are no longer made in a vacuum; rather, employees provide input, ideas, and solutions.

It was a long road, but we were able to take this company from funked up to fully functional and a whole lot more mindful.

BULLIES AND TOXIC PEEPS

Bullying isn't just something that happens in high school and teen movies like *Mean Girls*. Bullies—aka, utterly mindless people who suffer in a miserable and emotionally reactive existence—are everywhere, at every age and level of leadership.

Their self-awareness is, at best, low; their social awareness is non-existent; and they are deeply insecure and filled with self-loathing (unless they are true sociopaths or psychopaths, but that's a whole different can of tuna).

The Anti-Bullying Alliance defines "bullying" as: "the repetitive, intentional hurting of one person or group by another person or group, where the relationship involves an imbalance of power."[(1)] Bullies feel big by making others feel small, weak, hurt, or powerless.

Bullies' outward behaviors reflect their inward emotional struggles. Their behaviors have very little to do with you, and everything to do with their own misery. They've got lots of shadows to contend with and, counterintuitively, need massive doses of empathy. Remember Miranda? She had a whole attic full of shadows that she never confronted, and they filtered through her behavior at every turn.

Having said that, bullies are incredibly challenging to work with and require both mindfulness and a solid strategy to coach, redirect, or terminate.

The first question to ask is, "Can this person be coached?"

If so, a SMART plan is an ideal option. If you're unfamiliar with SMART, it's an acronym for Specific, Measurable, Attainable, Relevant, and Time-bound. Mapping out specific and exact expectations—including how you'll measure success, how your expectations fit in with their job, and by when the expectations need to be met—will either support everyone involved to succeed or provide the evidence necessary to make other decisions.

---

(1) https://anti-bullyingalliance.org.uk/tools-information/all-about-bullying/understanding-bullying/definition#

If for some reason the bully can't be coached, using a SMART plan will help you build your case for termination. Terminating people sucks, for real, but when the well-being of company culture is at stake, toxic people need to be released even if they are strong producers. (You can download a SMART planning guide at **www.unfunkyourselfbook.com**.)

But before you go sticking that "bully" label on everyone who pisses you off ...

Are you *really* dealing with someone who's toxic, or is this person simply challenging your comfort level, disagreeing with one of your policies, disrupting the status quo, or communicating in a style opposite to your own?

Impartiality is critical here—and that requires mindfulness. It can be incredibly difficult to be objective about someone we don't like and who pushes our buttons and triggers our insecurities. ASJs are often running the party when we perceive bullying or toxicity. For example, historically marginalized people—like women, BIPOC individuals, trans people, and neurodiverse folks—are labeled as difficult or toxic for requesting accommodations, equity, and inclusion via policy changes. The idea is that the squeaky wheel gets the grease—but all too often for marginalized people, the squeaky wheel is simply removed and replaced.

If human beings in your org are requesting equitable treatment, there is no need to remove them. Even if they are angry (and they may be, with good reason), they are not toxic bullies for requesting to be afforded opportunities that have historically been denied them. (Real quick note: equality and equity are not the same. Equality says that everyone has a desk; equity says everyone has a desk that suits their abilities and needs.)

GENERATIONAL DIFFERENCES

As I'm writing this in 2024, there are four generations working alongside each other: Baby Boomers, Gen-Xers, Millennials, and Gen-Zers. The Gen Alphas are fast approaching, and leaders everywhere need to learn to pivot to meet the needs of the folks they're recruiting.

I hear a lot of complaints about the different generations by all the different generations. As leaders, we fuel these complaints with our own assumptions, judgments, and misinformation. It makes sense: we've been sold the idea that each generation is irreconcilably different from the others, and that they all want vastly different things. In my many years of consulting and coaching, I haven't seen too much conflict come directly from generational issues, but it's a great soundbite: "Generational Conflict in The Workplace!" What I actually see more of is "Generational Similarities and Compromise in The Workplace" because, really, no matter our generation, we all want the same things at work: the ability to use our skills and talents, be productive, make a good living, and enjoy the work that we do. The struggles we face with those desires have less to do with generations and more to do with policies and pay rates.

That said, when other conflicts arise, generational differences in perspective and communication can add another layer of discomfort, fear, and cognitive dissonance.

In order to work with each other, we have to understand each other. In order to do that, we have to be willing to listen, learn, and believe. We must be empathetic.

So, let's unpack all the generational drama, because though the stereotypes contain some truth, they are only a single story, and much of the context is missing. Each generation was dealt a different hand to play by national and world events and economies. Some are much more challenging than others considering turbulent economic and workforce changes. Let's also remember that generations span fifteen to twenty years, so the various subsets within them are also different from each other.

Baby Boomers

Born between 1946 and 1964, this generation is stereotyped as being workaholics, greedy, stingy, conservative, bigoted, narrow-minded, and tech challenged.

Baby Boomers are a fascinating group. The children of Great Depression survivors, this group was birthed into the "New Middle Class"—a segment of society that did not exist in the United States before World War II. They understand, based on their parents' stories and experiences, how easily we can lose everything to market swings, war, or the luck of the draw. Therefore, this generation is more sensitive to holding on to things of value, like money, homes, antiques, etc.

Mid-career Baby Boomers experienced job growth and industry shifts, which for some brought wealth-building opportunities, and for others caused job loss and uncertainty.

In their formative years, Baby Boomers experienced civil unrest in many forms, including the Women's Rights and Civil Rights Movements, the Vietnam War, massive protests, violence, and widespread fear of both communism and nuclear annihilation. My friend's mom has described to her the "bomb drills" of the 1960s, where she and her elementary school classmates were taught how to shelter under desks and tables in case of a nuclear attack. There were also battles for and against integration of schools, with each side vehemently advocating for either tradition or progress. Societal norms of the time were being challenged, and Baby Boomers were striving for their own version of the American Dream. At the same time, technological advances brought television (and the TV news cycle) into every home; personal computers soon followed.

Baby Boomers are a hard-working generation because they didn't have a choice. They inherited pre-war ethics and work habits from their parents, and those were combined with a massive societal dose of both terror and opportunity. As we know, patterned behaviors are tough to break—and hard work has served many in this generation well.

Baby Boomers tend to be loyal to and proud of the companies they work for, often remaining with the same company and "climbing the ladder" to managerial positions. They value the positions they hold, since they've often worked long and hard to attain them, and also take pride in the duration of their tenure at their company. While the pension and benefits enjoyed by many of the early Baby Boomers are a thing of the past, the majority still consider it advisable to delay gratification and work toward retirement and its promised benefits. They value workplace visibility and may be reluctant remote workers, since a large part of their identity relies on how the company sees and values their work.

These people are our elders. They have been there, done that, and lived through what may be the most massive and radical societal shift in human history. They may have adjusted to tech with varying degrees of success, but their real contribution is their experience and wisdom. Younger generations should seek to learn from them about how things were, why they were that way, and what lessons were learned.

Be kind to your elders, my friend. They used to have to listen to baseball games on the radio.

Generation X (aka, Xers)

Born between 1965 and 1980, this generation is regarded as a posse of cynical slackers with bad attitudes, zero fucks to give, and no tolerance for bullshit. They can be hard workers if you leave them the hell alone, but start micromanaging and their already-minimal patience will wear out fast.

Often called the Lost Generation, these are the OG latchkey kids. As inflation rose and women gained more rights, more Baby Boomer moms entered the workforce to financially provide for their households. As both parents were often occupied with work and financial pressures, there was no one at home to meet the kids after school as had been the norm in decades past. Many kids were alone from the end of school until after dinner from the age of five or six onward. My Xer friends often say they raised themselves alongside their friends and siblings. Some admit to being more than slightly feral.

This generation experienced a sharp increase in divorce rates and split parenting, and soothed themselves with MTV, TV dinners, Atari, alt-rock, a splash of nihilism, and a foundational belief in their own self-sufficiency. Parents? Authority figures? Who needs those? We've got this.

During Gen-X's formative years, they were exposed to largely uncensored information related to global violence as 24-hour television became the norm. They fought in the first Iraq War, watched the Oklahoma City bombing and the fall of the Berlin Wall on live TV, and witnessed both the horror of the AIDS crisis and the additional horror of an apathetic governmental response. They also experienced global economic expansion and mass outsourcing, along with the resulting layoffs, reorgs, and restructuring. The "climb the ladder" approach of their parents' generation was no longer a viable strategy, so they learned instead to be flexible, adaptable, and a little bit cynical.

If you haven't guessed yet, trust—especially trust in authority—is an issue for Gen-Xers on several levels. They're also the most anxious generation. (Remember, humans are inherently uncomfortable with uncertainty, and Gen-X has lived with it since birth in a unique way.)

The result of all of these factors is a generation of fiercely independent and adaptable self-starters who seek diversity of skills and balance in their lives. They're tech-savvy but not overly tech-dependent. They figured it out, often the hard way, and because of that are highly entrepreneurial and free-thinking.

Gen-X is the current "sandwich" generation, raising children as well as caring for aging parents, so a healthy work/life balance is a high priority for them. They're also not as dedicated to work as their parents were. Most Xers don't want to sacrifice personal or family time for a company and are quick to leave organizations that don't meet their needs in this area.

If you want to know all about resilience, self-trust, thinking on your feet, the best way to eat SpaghettiOs, or how to open a beer with literally any random household object, find a Gen-Xer.

Generation Y (aka, Millennials)

Born between 1981 and 1996, this group is often accused of being lazy, entitled, difficult to work with, selfish, commitment-phobic, and too reliant on tech. They are the "participation trophy" generation.

Millennials make up more of the labor force right now than any other generation, but they are not the most engaged—in part because of the dynamics that shaped their approach to work, the workforce, and society in general.

Many members of this generation were raised by "helicopter parents" who took a hands-on approach to every aspect of parenting (and, some would argue, over-parenting). And yup, everyone got a trophy, or a ribbon, or a cookie—but the Millennials didn't give those things to themselves, Nope, we have young Boomers and older Gen-Xers to thank for that. Those parents knew what it felt like to be ignored, passed over, and excluded, and they wanted to make damn sure their kids didn't suffer that way.

This generation's childhood was violently disrupted by the September 11, 2001 attacks and the heightened fear and social divisiveness that followed. What's more, Millennials came into the workforce during and around the 2008 recession. Not only do they have the most student loan debt of any generation, but many couldn't find meaningful work or affordable housing after earning those coveted degrees. As a result, they have been slower to buy homes, start families, and "settle down" than their older peers.

This isn't laziness. It's simply pragmatism.

And, you know, math.

Despite what older generations may say, Millennials are resilient, self-aware, and persistent in their pursuit of meaningful and lucrative work. They're smart. They're educated. They know their worth. And, thanks to those participation trophies, they know that showing up matters just as much as winning. As a group, they're far more effective communicators than their older peers, and far more willing to change behaviors that offend or challenge others.

If you want to know the perfect angle for a selfie, find the best meme for any life crisis, or master the fine art of making life look easier, cooler, and more profitable than it probably is, ask a Millennial, they'll know.

Oh, and don't forget to hashtag. #theyinventedit #nofilter #actuallyyesfilter

Generation Z (aka, Zoomers)

Born between 1996 and 2012, this cohort is believed to be entitled, impatient, poor communicators who are too reliant on tech, have unrealistic expectations, and generally don't want to work.

However, Gen-Zers are incredibly pragmatic, shift seamlessly with rapidly changing technological advances, and are honed-in on global issues and socio-political turmoil. They are social justice warriors, often hyper-focused on climate, fair trade, and sustainability. They will call someone out on their hypocrisy and bullshit *immediately*—and probably also on TikTok.

As a group, they have a strong desire to do good things in the world, and seek work that not only matters to them but matters to their communities and the planet as a whole. They desire flexibility in the workplace and are not tolerant of rigidity or authoritarian cultures.

They also just want to be *happy*.

As for being tech-obsessed … well, blame the Xers who birthed them. Tech as a lifestyle was just beginning to take hold when this generation was born, and let me tell you from personal experience, it's a lot easier as a busy working mom (or dad) to give your kid your phone or tablet when they won't stop crying at the restaurant than it is to cancel the order and pack up the baby. These kids literally grew up with screens in their faces.

We're still learning about the dynamics of Gen-Z in the workplace and the contributions they make, but if you want to go viral, cancel someone, or use five screens at once without breaking a sweat, ask a Zoomer.

POWER STRUGGLES

We can't talk about leadership without discussing notions of power.

If you occupy any kind of management or supervisory role, you are in a position of power. You may not be the CEO, but if you are listed above other people on an org chart or given budgetary discretion, you have power.

There are three types of power to consider when we discuss leadership. All are necessary at some point or another, and they all work together. Your job as a leader is to determine—using social awareness and emotional intelligence—what is the best time to wield each type of power.

POWER OVER

This is the most common understanding of power. When we hear phrases like military power, financial power, political power, this is the type of power we imagine. It is a domineering power that relies on fear, and also on force. In the workplace, it's a "do as I say with no questions asked or else" sort of power. It often comes with a hint (or an overt threat) of humiliation, demotion, or termination if the conditions of those in power are not met or exceeded.

With few exceptions, this is *not* the best use of power when working with other humans. The only exceptions are legal restrictions and true emergencies. If someone is stealing from the company, sexually harassing other employees, or scamming old ladies from the company laptop, and you have irrefutable proof, feel free to get authoritarian on their ass (with proper procedure, documentation, and clear communication, of course). If there's a fire in the building, you should absolutely shout, "Everyone out, NOW!" But exercising that latitude over a missed deadline or a minor employee dispute? That's a no-go.

Another example of "power over" is micromanagement. Unlike an authoritarian attitude, this often comes from a place of honest caring. The problem is, it's caring about the wrong thing. For example, if one of your reports is having a tough time understanding or completing a task, you might think, "Ugh, again? I'll just do it myself." This makes sense, because you know how to do the task, and it takes so darn long to teach people stuff. You want it done right for the sake of the company or your customer, so you step in, take over, get it done, and that's that.

However, I want you to think about a time when this happened to you. Maybe you were a kid trying to paint your bedroom wall, but you were being "too messy," so your dad took the roller and did it himself. Or, maybe this happened in your early career, or even as you took on a leadership role. Sure, the task got done, and done well, because your boss knew how to do the thing … but what did you learn? Probably nothing. You also probably felt undermined, minimized, and full of self-doubt. Maybe your productivity slipped. Maybe you lost trust in your boss, or your own abilities.

Simon Sinek reminds us that "taking care of those in our charge" means taking the time—making the time—to actually help people understand how to do the things we expect of them.

POWER TO

Part of being a leader is managing your energy and time well so you can allocate them to bigger and more important tasks. Therefore, good leaders are smart about delegating work. "Power to" is basically delegation of duties to professionally develop people. More than that, it's an empowerment tool that demonstrates trust in the abilities of the folks to whom you are delegating.

One of your many jobs as a leader is to develop the next generation of leaders. If you're not already, you should become acutely familiar with your reports' professional desires. What are their strengths? Where do they need additional support, education, or development? What do they want to learn? What do they want to stay away from? How can you help mentor them as they create the next iteration of their careers?

What are the smaller responsibilities you carry that can be strategically delegated to your reports for their benefit? For example, if you know that someone is interested in becoming a leader in your organization (or any organization), consider allowing them to take a peripheral role in your management activities. Perhaps you could invite them to be part of the budgeting process to kickstart their understanding of back-end operations.

"Power to" builds trust between you and another individual and strengthens the entire organization.

POWER WITH

Some leaders get stuck in a trap of thinking they need to know everything and call all the shots. This is fearful and counterproductive thinking. As a leader, you are rarely the smartest person in the room, nor should you be. You've hired all these incredibly smart and capable people, so let them shine!

According to Steve Jobs, late CEO and Founder of Apple, "It doesn't make sense to hire smart people and tell them what to do; we hire smart people so they can tell *us* what to do." "Power with" builds trust among teams. Innovation happens when people are given space and permission to think, be creative, bounce ideas off one another, and fail forward.

HEALTHY CONFLICT

Trust is necessary to have healthy conflict. Following the suggestions in the previous sections will minimize unhealthy and unnecessary conflict. Combining good communication strategies with emotional intelligence and self-management will set the stage for conflicts to be handled in a healthy way.

Like I mentioned before, conflict doesn't have to feel yucky or have an angry undertone. Is conflict uncomfortable? Sure. But the status quo is no friend to creativity. Innovation, growth, and creativity are born out of discomfort, need, or both. Some degree of conflict is required to spur us to new heights. When it's managed well, it doesn't need to be stressful.

"Healthy conflict" refers to disagreements or disputes that are managed mindfully and constructively (so simmer down, amygdala!) so that they can foster growth, understanding, and positive outcomes. Healthy conflict requires a few ingredients. Luckily, if you're leading mindfully, these things aren't a big deal.

First and foremost, all participants in a debate must agree to treat each other with respect, even when they disagree; manage their emotions so that they can remain calm and composed; and avoid deliberately escalating the conflict. In real time, that means no name-calling, personal attacks, or disrespectful behavior like eye rolling, *tsk*ing, or huffy sighs.

Second, all sides should be able to express their views openly and honestly, and also listen actively to each other's perspectives. Remember, almost all workplace conflict is centered around specific issues or problems rather than personal characteristics or behaviors, and it's only when we are reacting mindlessly that we leverage those characteristics and behaviors as "reasons" for the issues. And the goal is to find a mutually acceptable solution. All sides must be willing to compromise and collaborate to reach a resolution.

Third, feedback should be an important part of the

discussion and also be given in a way that is constructive and aimed at improvement rather than criticism. The purpose of feedback is to understand the underlying interests and needs of both parties, not just their stated positions.

When these elements are present in combination, healthy conflict can lead directly to innovation, improved decision-making, and stronger relationships as it encourages diverse perspectives and problem-solving.

MANAGING HEATED MOMENTS

Still feeling conflicted about conflict? Not to worry. I've developed a step-by-step process to support you to mindfully navigate conflictual or challenging situations and conversations.

Here are the three steps to mindfully managing conflict:

- *Identify what's happening and what you're feeling* (self-awareness)
- *Recognize Hot Zone tendencies* (self-awareness and social awareness)
- *Take control* (self-management and relationship management)

Step #1: Identify What's Happening and What You're Feeling (Self-Awareness)

How do you know what you're feeling when you're feeling it? That may sound like a silly question because we think we know what we're feeling when we feel it, but when we're stressed or triggered, sometimes the feelings are too intense and complex to pinpoint.

Lucky for all of us, a team of innovative Finnish scientists led by Dr. Lauri Nummenmaa, Director of the Human Emotion Systems laboratory at Turku PET Centre and Department of Psychology, University of Turku, developed a body heat map to show how people feel different emotions on their bodies.[(2)]

There are a multitude of cool things about the research and the associated visuals, notably that, even across cultures, human emotions are incredibly similar. We physically respond to emotional stimuli, and as leaders we can therefore approach other humans knowing that if we trigger a certain emotion, we will also trigger a certain physical response, which is similar to our own physical response. This gives new meaning to, "I know how you feel."

This experiment also demonstrated that the mind and the body are not even remotely separate; rather, they are intimately entwined. Emotional health and physical health are reliant on one another—which brings a new level of urgency to supporting our teams' mental health, as well as our own.

You can check out the body heat map image on the Resources page at **www.unfunkyourselfbook.com**.

Step #2: Recognize Hot Zone Tendencies (Self-Awareness and Social Awareness)

When you get triggered, what is your go-to response? Are you a yeller? A retreater? A cold-shoulderer? A placator? A thrower? Recognizing your trends and patterns is key to managing yourself in the moment.

---

(2) Nummenmaa, L., Glerean, E., Hari, R., & Hietanen, J. K. (2014). Bodily maps of emotions. Proceedings of the National Academy of Sciences, 111(2), 646-651. https://doi.org/10.1073/pnas.1321664111

Whenever you're triggered, your first step is to check yourself ASAP. Whatever your response is, pull it back. Once you determine the emotion you're feeling, you can acknowledge the pattern and then disrupt it.

Don't be fooled into thinking this is easy. It's not. But it is totally possible, and the more you do it, the easier it gets. And the best part is, it doesn't take long to see the results—and your success will push you to try even harder.

Step #3: Take Control (self-management and relationship management)

There are two parts to taking control in conflict: manage the pause and flip the script.

Manage the Pause

If you're feeling triggered, it's best not to react in the moment. You need to give your amygdala time to settle down and allow the rest of your brain to start reasoning again. So, take a beat, pause, work yourself back into your logical brain, and then respond.

In case you need it, here's an all-purpose, all-situation script. "I need a few minutes. I'll get back to you." Apply it liberally in meetings, on phone calls, on video conferences, by the water cooler, and literally anywhere else you might encounter a conflict.

If the other person is the one triggered, they may not pause, so offer the pause to them. "It seems like right now is not a good time to have this discussion. Let's regroup in ten minutes so we can have a productive discussion."

The pause goes for emails as well. It's *never* a good idea to send a hot email. You can't take it back, and the glaring evidence of your Hot Zone will live forever on the company servers.

In heated email situations, I recommend the following:

- *Reply to the sender with a simple, "Thank you for your email. I will respond shortly," or something similar.* This way, you've acknowledged receipt of the email, but you've also given yourself time to craft a mindful, non-emotional response.
- *Open your journal, a Word doc, or the Notes app on your phone, and write out everything you want to say.* The emotions you are feeling are valid, and writing is a great way to process feelings. That said, remember that digital communication doesn't include tone or body language, so once you're calmer, consider whether you might have been misinterpreting or making assumptions.
- *Once you've written your retort, save it, close it, and return to it in a few hours.* At that point you should be able to rewrite it as a logical response, even if you are still angry. Strip out any accusations, assumptions, judgments, or Bad Info. Keep to the facts. If possible, try to accommodate the other person's communication style in your response so that they understand and can process it easily.

- *If the issue is time-sensitive, send your reply at this point.* However, if possible, it's best to sleep on your email and re-read it again after a full day has passed and you are no longer in the Hot Zone.

Flip the Script

This tactic requires some serious mindfulness and restraint. So, let's get psychologically nerdy for a minute.

The human brain contains a special type of neurons, called mirror neurons, that fire when we observe and imitate others' behavior. For example, yawns are not actually contagious; rather we are imitating a behavior that someone else has performed that triggered our mirror neurons. The same thing happens when we see or hear someone laugh and we find ourselves chuckling. Mirror neurons are a mechanism of connection, learning, and empathy.

If, during a conflict, our opponent starts to emotionally escalate by raising their voice, widening their physical stance, invading our personal space, or demonstrating aggressive facial expressions—our mirror neurons will fire, and our norm will be to meet their escalation. "I see your personal space invasion. I'll raise you a pair of clenched fists!" In these moments, your amygdala is fully engaged and is preparing your body to fight, flee, or freeze.

The traditional script is to either escalate right along with your opponent to see who can be more aggressive, or back down to placate the opponent (which looks and feels like admitting weakness or defeat). The strategic and mindful "flip" response is to remain calm yet still engaged.

Yes, the other person is escalating, and the drive to match them is strong. But you don't have to give in. Think about a time you lashed out from your Hot Zone. Were you in control? Nope. Where was your power? In the hands of the person who pissed you off! Furthermore, just like you don't want to work for a hothead who loses their temper at the drop of a hat, neither do your reports. So don't be the hothead.

When you maintain calm in the face of your opponent's Hot Zone fire, they will realize the need to deescalate or risk looking like a complete fool—because as they escalate and you don't, an element of confusion is introduced. They will soon realize that they have handed their power over to you. You can then introduce a solution, or simply suggest a break, from a place of control.

In the animal kingdom, the loudest and fiercest dominate. In the human workplace, calm and centered wins the game.

UN-FUNKING FEEDBACK

I am often asked for guidance on how to provide tough feedback, and how to handle redirection conversations. There is no perfect answer and no perfect approach, but I can offer some guidelines that should help the conversation proceed as well as possible.

Before we begin, a few quick reminders.

- *People are emotional before they are logical.* Using these transparent tactics will decrease amygdala reaction (Hot Zone) and increase thoughtful response (Cool Zone).

- *The problem is not the problem.* The problem is your attitude about the problem. So, neutralize your headspace before diving into the conversation lest your ASJs decide to join the party uninvited.
- *Mind your approach and communication style.* Make sure you are meeting the needs of the person to whom you are providing feedback. Your way may not be the right way for them.
- *Don't assume intent.* Allow yourself to hear the other person's reasons and solutions.
- *Never attribute to malice what is adequately explained by ignorance.* 'Nuff said.

All of us know what it feels like to receive unsolicited feedback that sounds canned and one-sided. Yuck. You can absolutely do better. Feedback conversations should go along the following lines to keep everyone calm and in their logical brains.

1. *Make sure the person is open to hearing feedback.* Unsolicited feedback can feel threatening and elicit emotionally charged reactions. The easiest way to get permission is just to ask.
2. *Explain why you're giving the feedback.*
3. *Deliver the feedback transparently and succinctly, with no ASJs or accusations.* Avoid the "compliment sandwich" (compliment/criticism/compliment) approach as that

can feel disingenuous. Just take a breath and trust yourself. When you do, your delivery will be clearer and less emotional, and the conversation will stay on track.

4. *Listen to the person's response to the feedback.* If they think it is unfair, ask them to explain why. If the person is heading toward the Hot Zone, remember to stay calm and engaged.
5. *Ask them what questions they have for you.* Answer all questions before you conclude the discussion.
6. *Set new expectations based on the conversation.*

Here's a helpful little example:

1. "I would like to share some observations and am wondering if you're open to some feedback."
2. "To make sure that you're set up for success, I need to set/reset expectations."
3. "The email that you sent this morning has caused confusion and concern among our volunteers. I'd like to approach this conversation by sharing what I observed that raised concerns and get your view of the situation. From there we can determine a solution to this current situation and adjust for future communications."

4. "It's possible that I may be misunderstanding something or may have even contributed to the issue at hand. Let's discuss the situation."
5. "Do you have any questions for me, or does anything in this conversation feel unclear or unresolved to you?"
6. "Based on what we've discussed, I think that we're in agreement on the following expectations ..."

If this seems like a completely weird way to go about giving feedback, good. It's not standard, and it's not what we're used to. But it is the most effective, honest, and transparent method of providing feedback that will be heard, acknowledged, and appreciated.

UN-FUNKING YOUR CONFLICT MANAGEMENT

ASK FOR FEEDBACK

As a leader, you want to provide feedback to your reports to help them succeed. But feedback is a two-way street, and you should request the same of them. You have no way of knowing if you're a good leader or a Funked-Up Boss unless you ask (and actually listen to) the people who work for and with you.

This is definitely not the norm in leadership culture, but since you picked up this book and read to this point, you obviously want to be a better leader, and the specifics of how to fine-tune your mindfulness will always need to come from the people who experience your mindlessness.

When I bring this up in workshops and ask how many leaders seek feedback from their reports, I am usually answered by a lot of awkward shifting and notebook flipping. When I ask why they don't seek feedback, I often hear, "It's just not something that we do." When I ask why not, I don't usually get a straight answer. Instead, what typically surfaces is fear.

"I'm afraid of what they'll say," is one common thought. To which I respond, "Well, how are you going to be a better boss if you don't know what you need to do better?"

Honestly, it's so important to open your mind to the various areas of leadership where you can improve. Your ego doesn't want to hear that you're not perfect and successful in every single way; it's fragile and afraid, and it hates being called out. But the mindful approach is to welcome feedback, clarify comments, and make adjustments to meet the requests of your colleagues and reports.

How cool would it have been if, when you were beginning your career, one of your Funked-Up Bosses asked you, "Hey, do you have some feedback to share with me about my leadership?" And, how cool would it have been if they took your feedback and actually made meaningful changes to their leadership approach? You would have been happier, and they would have been a better boss.

Fear of retaliation holds many people back from providing feedback to their bosses, but when those bosses approach feedback in a smart and genuine way, such as via an anonymous 360 review, employees are more apt to be honest.

Once you receive feedback (and you've had time to move

out of the Hot Zone and into your logical brain), thank your team for their input. Highlight the trends and issues you see in the feedback, and then share the steps you will take to remedy those issues. Then, *actually follow through* with the changes you've promised, even if you do so imperfectly.

Survey the group again in six months to see how you're doing, just as you'd do if they had been the ones being evaluated.

Does this make you uncomfortable? Why?

Does this sound like a good plan? Why?

360 EVALS

A 360-degree evaluation (or 360 Eval) requests feedback from an employee's peers, direct reports, managers, and sometimes even clients. It's a good idea to use both quantitative rating (scale from 1 to 5) and qualitative opportunities (long or short paragraph) to capture performance and nuances. Listed below are some well-rounded categories and sample questions you could use to design an effective 360 evaluation for yourself or a team member.

Leadership and Management

- How effectively does [Name] lead and inspire their team?
- How well does [Name] communicate a clear vision or direction?
- Does [Name] make fair and balanced decisions?

- How effectively does [Name] handle conflicts within the team?

Communication Skills

- How effectively does [Name] communicate information to others?
- Is [Name] approachable and open to feedback?
- How well does [Name] listen and understand others' perspectives?
- Does [Name] provide clear instructions and expectations?

Collaboration and Teamwork

- How well does [Name] work with colleagues across departments?
- Does [Name] support others in achieving team goals?
- How effectively does [Name] contribute to team discussions and decision-making?
- Does [Name] encourage others to share ideas and opinions?

Adaptability and Problem-Solving

- How well does [Name] adapt to change and uncertainty?
- How effectively does [Name] solve problems and find creative solutions?

- Does [Name] remain calm and professional under pressure?
- Is [Name] open to new ideas and approaches?

Accountability and Dependability

- Does [Name] follow through on commitments?
- How well does [Name] take responsibility for their actions?
- Is [Name] reliable and punctual?
- Does [Name] hold themselves accountable for achieving goals?

Technical Skills and Job Knowledge

- How proficient is [Name] in their role's technical skills?
- Does [Name] keep their knowledge up-to-date in their field?
- How effectively does [Name] use tools and resources to complete tasks?
- Does [Name] demonstrate a good understanding of their job responsibilities?

Client and Customer Focus

- How well does [Name] understand and meet client or customer needs?
- Does [Name] communicate effectively with clients and customers?

- How responsive is [Name] to client or customer feedback?
- How well does [Name] represent the company's values to clients?

Growth and Development

- Does [Name] actively seek feedback for improvement?
- How effectively does [Name] pursue professional growth opportunities?
- Does [Name] show a willingness to learn new skills?
- How well does [Name] set and work toward personal and professional goals?

CHAPTER NINE

HIRING AND ONBOARDING

MY FIRST JOB AFTER leaving the nonprofit world was as a project manager at a wellness company. The job required significant detail orientation, focus, and deep documentation.

My friend, I am an Assertive/Inspiring style. Like, a big ol' A/I with a tiny splash of Logical. I am not detail-oriented in the least. I'm a big-picture, vision-and-reach thinker.

This was *not* the ideal role for me.

The person who hired me, also an Assertive/Inspiring style, really liked my personality. We quickly connected, and I made her laugh, so she thought I'd be an excellent culture fit. She was right on that count; I fit in really well with the team and was like a little ray of happiness in the building.

But again: I *sucked* at this job.

I vividly remember sitting with my boss and expressing my concerns that I wasn't doing a great job in my role.

She responded by saying, "Emily, you may not be great at the work, but people really like you!"

"Yeah, but I'm terrible at the job, and people won't like me for long if I can't do the work well."

I bowed out of the role shortly thereafter. The person hired to replace me was absolutely a fit: detail-oriented, data-driven, and precise. They weren't the life of the party, but that's not what the role called for, so they succeeded in a manner that I did not.

MINDLESS HIRING CREATES MINDLESS STRUGGLE

The hiring process, though often structured with the best intentions, is rife with human flaws. There's a lot to consider when you're hiring new folks onto your team and into the company, and much of it ties into everything we've discussed so far in this book—in particular, identities (yours and your hires'), ASJs, communication styles, and general mindfulness.

Like my former boss in the story above, many of us tend to hire people who are like us—people we click with and who "get us." This means that, without mindfulness in the equation, we can end up with a team we love to hang out with but who struggle to fulfill day-to-day expectations.

In essence, this comes back to tribe mentality. We *like* being with people who are like us. For example, as an Assertive/Inspiring style, it can be frustrating as heck for me to try to communicate deliverables and expectations to a Logical person who needs all the details. I mean, most of the time, *I* don't even have the details, so how the heck can I give them to my team? If I'm not mindful, this frustration can easily translate into feelings and judgments like, "That person is *so* difficult," or "They just don't get it! Maybe they're not a good fit for the team."

Unchecked tribe mentality can result in an imbalanced team and lopsided delivery. Having a team full of one or two communication styles might feel good, but it rarely produces good results. I've had many, many coaching conversations in which managers lament the fact that Employee X, who is "*so* freaking great," isn't performing well and they don't know what to do to fix it. Nine times out of ten, these managers have hired based on personal affinity and not actual compatibility for the role. The result is a communication gap and/or style issue that affects the employee's ability to deliver.

This is not to say that culture fit isn't important. It is. But someone can be a good culture fit and still be very different from us in terms of approach and communication style. Tribal thinking and culture awareness are not the same thing.

No amount of hard work and perseverance will ever make me good at details. My Assertive/Inspiring communication style and love of the big picture are integral to who I am. If I had stayed in that role, not only would the team and my boss eventually have lost patience with and confidence in me, but I would also likely have started to doubt my own capacity and been miserable to boot.

Funked-up hiring hurts everyone.

The antidote, of course, is mindfulness.

So, when considering a new hire, start by assessing which communication style(s) will be the best fit for the role. If that style makes you uncomfortable for any reason or doesn't "click" with you, keep that in mind for later.

Next, ask yourself what the expectations for the role are. What will a candidate be expected to produce in this position, and what skill sets will help them succeed? Make sure the job description you put out is specific and clear. It's hard to meet expectations if those expectations are blurry! If you can, give examples of the types of work that will be done so candidates are better educated before applying and can self-select for the role.

When you're constructing the interview process, keep in mind that you can also ask candidates to provide their own take on the role and the expectations therein. This helps you understand not only how folks are reading the job description, but also where their skills and interests lie, which can help you ensure a good fit.

After you're clear on those two items—style fit and expectations—you can go on to vetting candidates. This is where you really have to keep your ASJs in check, both with regard to communication styles and in a broader sense as well. There are reasons why certain questions (how old are you, do you have children, what is your sexual orientation) cannot legally be asked of candidates. Demographic information almost always has some bias attached to it. Women are often coached to remove their wedding rings prior to interviews because there is a bias about married women being distracted by children and household responsibilities.

To discover whether your concerns about a potential hire are genuine (role fit, a skills or experience gap, or a mismatch in terms of communication style) or if they're really coming from your Notorious ASJs, ask yourself the following questions:

- Do I *know* this, or do I *think* this?
- What evidence do I have to support this thought as it applies to this particular candidate?

If you only think something, or it's attached to an ASJ, you've landed in an amygdala trap, and you need to get out ASAP.

Actually, you should be asking the above questions if you're super excited about a potential candidate, too! If you feel like you've found a "soul colleague" without ever having experienced them at work, or you just "have a good feeling" about this person without any real proof to support your enthusiasm, that's a red flag for tribal thinking.

You may also need to contend with the ASJs of another member of the hiring team. Walking someone else through their biases is a delicate operation, and great care should be taken lest their amygdala fire up and spark unnecessary conflict. If you notice that ASJs are afoot, gently challenge your colleague by providing your merit- and evidence-based notes about the candidate. (And you can always slip them this book!)

If you're an HR leader and a department manager sends over a description of a potential candidate, read through it, note the ambiguous parts, and then seek clarification. With a little practice, you can spot ASJs a mile away.

THE NEW KID ON THE PLAYGROUND

Starting a new job, although exciting, is also scary and stressful for many, if not most, people. Essentially, you're the new kid at school. You don't know where to go, who to talk to, or who will let you sit at the lunch table with them.

As a candidate, the job description and the company are easy enough to research (especially if the job description is thorough and accurate, as I've advised above). The culture and team dynamics? Not so much.

When onboarding any new hire, whether they're entry-level or upper management, remember that 75 percent of learning is social and emotional. When you can discover their communication style quickly—for example, by requiring a Communication Compass assessment as part of your onboarding process—you can adapt their training to their needs. You can also simply ask your new hire what learning tools are best for their style and then do what you can to provide them.

The big lesson in mindful onboarding is that one size does not fit all—not even close. I'm sure your HR team has put together a brilliantly packaged toolkit (likely based on their own learning styles), but that doesn't mean its application should be set in stone. The last thing you want when bringing on a new team member is to be constantly pivoting around misunderstandings, confusion, and frustrations.

Once the technical aspects of onboarding are complete, it will be time to integrate your new hire into the established team and company culture.

Team cohesion requires trust, which requires comfort, which requires intentional connection and the application of emotional intelligence. Create a culture of welcoming and appreciation so that the shock of the new role and new environment is lessened. You can also set up getting-to-know-you meetings (which I recommend doing over food, because I am an A/I style and also a foodie, but I digress). Teams work best when each member knows the strengths of the others so they can complement each other, not compete with one another.

All of this is very big-picture, which you will likely be fine with if you're an Assertive, Inspiring, or Collaborative communication style, and may not love if you're Logical or Supportive. But the truth is, there is no one way to hire and onboard mindfully. Your job is always going to be to get to know your new hire, learn their communication style, and ask what their needs are in relation to both their role and to team cohesion. It's truly an individualized process—but when done with intention and emotional intelligence, this approach will support you to build a positive culture for the whole team.

MINDLESS FIRING CREATES MINDLESS DRAMA ... AND POTENTIAL LAWSUITS

Except in cases of blatant bad behavior—like embezzlement, violence, harassment, or playing Hanson's "MMMBop" on repeat at their desk—firing someone needs to be a deeply mindful process.

It's imperative to make sure you have all your proverbial ducks in a row when considering firing someone. If any of those ducks are your own or others' ASJs, and/or you have not attempted *every* method of training, re-training, and expectation-setting, it's time to reconsider what you're planning before you end up in legal hot water.

As Ice Cube wisely warns, "You better check yo'self before you wreck yo'self."

Prepare carefully to ensure that your decision to let this person go is based on clear, well-documented reasoning. Even in at-will states, lawyers are hesitant to take a case that smells like discrimination of any kind.

Next, plan the conversation ahead of time by writing out exactly what you will say to the employee. Practice and refine it. Anticipate your employee's potential reactions, since you'd better believe that their amygdala dimmer switch will be switched on and pushed up high. Yours will, too, and if you're not mindful you may find yourself becoming preemptively defensive.

Firing someone sucks. It sucks for them, it sucks for you, and it just all-around sucks. That's why empathy matters so much here. You've probably been fired/let go before, so you know how shitty it feels. It's an embarrassing blow to the ego, and the feeling of failure and shame floods right up. So, be kind and respectful. Avoid harsh language and blunt words, instead choosing clear and firm language that preserves the person's dignity.

Also, *do not fire anyone via email or chat*. Ever. It may seem ridiculous that I need to write this particular suggestion, but you'd be surprised how often it happens. It is an inhumane, lazy, weak, and cowardly method. Leadership is hard, and firing people is one of a hard job's hardest aspects. Don't funk it up by chickening out and resorting to email.

Conduct the meeting in person and in a neutral, respectful space, ensuring privacy so that no one feels humiliated. Allow time for the person to process, and invite dialogue as you provide honest feedback as to why this decision was necessary. Be kind, but don't sugarcoat. That's just as yucky as being mean.

If the termination is due to a skills lack, be honest, and then do your best to provide ideas and resources related to what a good fit might be, or information on how to obtain the skills necessary to do the work.

Lastly, allow for a graceful exit. If possible, let them share the news of their departure with their colleagues instead of broadcasting it on the company chat. Allow them some say in how/why they leave the company. Once the person has exited, debrief with their colleagues (because their own dimmer switches will go on, no question) but maintain confidentiality and respect at all times.

By approaching the situation mindfully, you will not only maintain the dignity of the person being let go but also uphold a culture of respect and care within your organization.

UN-FUNK YOUR HIRING

These journal prompts encourage self-awareness and strategic thinking, ensuring each hire aligns with the needs and vision of the organization, not anyone's ASJs.

Define the Role and Fit

- What core qualities am I looking for in this role, beyond skills and experience? Why are these qualities essential for the team and company culture?
- What challenges might this new hire face in the role, and what qualities or skills would help them navigate these challenges?
- What values do my team hold, and how can a new hire complement or enhance this dynamic?

Evaluate for Potential, Not Just Experience

- What soft skills would support success in this role over the long term, even if they're not immediately apparent on a resume?

- How can I evaluate candidates for adaptability and a willingness to learn?
- What past experiences could demonstrate a candidate's resilience or growth mindset?

Reduce Unconscious Bias

- What unconscious biases might I bring to the hiring process?
- How can I ensure that my evaluation criteria remain focused on relevant qualities and not stereotypes or assumptions?
- What steps can I take to standardize my evaluation across candidates to promote fairness?
- How could this candidate bring a unique perspective or valuable diversity to our team?

Envision Success and Growth

- What does success look like in this role in six months, one year, and beyond?
- How can I ensure this role provides a meaningful opportunity for the candidate's growth as well as ours?
- What support and resources can I provide to help this new hire feel integrated, empowered, and valued?

Reflect on Your Own Hiring Intentions

- What assumptions am I making about this role or the type of person who should fill it?
- How can I remain open-minded and flexible about unexpected qualities or qualifications that may be valuable?
- What lessons have I learned from past hiring experiences that can inform this one?
- What steps will I take to assess and support this individual's long-term job satisfaction and sense of purpose in our organization?

CHAPTER TEN

LIVING AND LEADING UN-FUNKED

WHEN I FIRST MET QUITA, she was entangled in an emotional web of perceived rejection and judgment, and squarely seated in the Hot Zone.

She considered herself a "nice" person until she had to be otherwise, but because she was preemptively defensive most of the time, she needed to be "otherwise" often. She very much had a "look what you made me do" mentality about both the people who reported to her and the people to whom she reported.

It was *so* Orange Zone.

"Super sus," as the kids would say.

A Logical/Supportive style, Quita was focused on quality and precision, ensuring that policies were followed to the letter. As a result, she felt undermined when upper leadership let things slide or changed policies "for no reason" (her words).

However, she didn't want to cause disharmony, so she didn't voice her concerns or opinions, nor did she offer suggestions. Instead, she stewed in her dissatisfaction, which ended up trickling down into her teams. This dissatisfaction presented as a snippy tone of voice, impatient redirection, and avoidance of the people who she felt had betrayed her.

Her standard line was, "Everything is fine." Then, she'd lose all rizz. Cringe.

When we began our work together, the first step was to help her become more mindful. At that point, she saw everything as a challenge to order and her own authority—and also probably an insult. Her amygdala perceived everything as a threat.

She came by this predisposition to confrontation honestly, she explained, as she was rarely supported by her family. She was made to feel like she never did anything right, and that no one was ever proud of her. Yeah, Quita had some big ol' boxes in her attic that were leaking all sorts of toxins into her work relationships. She was failing *all* vibe checks, bruh. (Okay, I'm having *way* too much fun with the Gen-Z slang.)

We worked on the root causes of her defensiveness and examined how she defined conflict. Then, we did some significant de-catastrophizing work, reflecting on her lifelong patterned behaviors of assumption and avoidance. Then, we looked for a practice that could help her maintain her new level of awareness on a daily basis.

Luckily, Quita already liked to journal. As a process thinker and a Logical/Supportive style, she needs to write out her thoughts and feelings to fully understand them. Then, she can set intentions to move through the blocks she encounters. However, her previous journal entries were long lists of grievances and *all* the ASJs, so we needed to shift how she was using her journaling time. I encouraged her to spend less paper space on what happened and more on how she was feeling about it and why.

In our subsequent check-ins, Quita told me that she was doing really well and that she had "gotten it"—as though she was solving a calculus problem. Then, in the next conversation, she'd tell me that she'd "messed up," or that she was struggling with certain people.

I totally understood. For folks who live their lives through to-do lists, the fluidity and endlessness of a mindfulness journey can be uncomfortable and a bit challenging to move into.

But, as Quita proved, not impossible.

After a while, she got better at noticing when she was in the Hot Zone, when she was hanging with the ASJs, and when she was reacting out of a sense of being triggered rather than responding to a genuine problem. When I spoke to her just the other day, she mentioned that her family keeps telling her how much happier she looks and sounds—which was *huge*, as they're not big on compliments.

"I am still journaling," she said, "and reading the books you suggested. I'm feeling so much more at peace, and my whole team is functioning better. I will never stop improving myself!"

"Get it, girl!" I hollered. "This is what it's all about!"

I know I've said it before, but I'll say it again: mindfulness is a lifelong journey. No one is at their best all the time, so as you evolve your mindful leader practice, remember that having a few mindless moments along the way is completely normal, to be expected, and not to be judged. I think we sometimes forget that there is beauty and opportunity in messing up. Reflection is part of the journey.

HOW'S THAT FUNK DOING, FRIEND?

Wow, we've come a long way since we started this journey together.

How are you doing so far? Has this information resonated with you?

Have you taken time to jot down your thoughts as you read? If not, now is a great time to pause and try it. (Are you a newbie? Get your handy guide to mindful journaling at **www.unfunkyourselfbook.com**.)

Because we are all different, and our reason(s) for and journeys into mindfulness are different, there is no such thing as perfection. In fact, I'd argue that there's no such thing as perfection anywhere in life (unless we're talking about sweet guitar riffs, in which case may I present Prince Rogers Nelson. I will die on this hill. Thank you.)

So, if there is no attainable "perfection" or ideal of mindfulness, and therefore no concrete end point for the journey, how did Quita and so many of my other clients get clarity about and commit to their own processes of un-funking themselves?

The truth is, they all had their own reasons, and so they all came to it differently. But all of my successful clients have three things in common: intention, commitment, and humility.

Let's look at each of those qualities separately.

INTENTION

Setting intentions provides you with some control over your emotions, especially if you're feeling stressed and busy. Intentional interactions with yourself and others are the key to mindful communication, self-compassion, empathy, understanding, and connection. They are also the key to un-funking your leadership and becoming a more mindful person.

Setting intentions is different than writing a to-do list.

To-do lists help us organize the tasks we need to accomplish. Setting intentions helps us organize the emotional space we will occupy while we accomplish those tasks—and, in the case of leaders, the emotional space you will hold while you guide your team(s) to accomplish their tasks.

It's always a good idea to make sure you're focused and grounded before setting intentions, as intentions set in a frazzled, exhausted, or cranky state will likely include lovely bits of ASJs and amygdala input. Instead, do your favorite practice to get grounded, and then make deliberate note of how you wish to approach your day.

You can ask yourself questions like:

- "What kind of energy will I need to present today?"
- "With whom will I meet, and how do I feel about them? Why do I feel that way? What are their learning, communication, and connection needs?"
- "How will I meet others' needs while also meeting my own?"
- "How will I maintain a thoughtful approach should I be irritated by a conversation?"
- "Am I feeling nervous about anything I have going on today?"

Invest the time to set your mind for the day so that you can be more fluid and adaptable—and, ultimately, more mindful.

Meditate, Breathe, Move, Write, Speak

There is no right or wrong way to set intentions, however, intentions are always more effective when they're set in a grounded, calm, and mindful place.

So, how do you get grounded?

I find that certain practices are consistently helpful for my clients. These practices can help you get grounded and feel "even-keel" so you can set your intentions and make a plan for your day without any mindless reactivity or attic gunk creeping in.

For some people, meditation is a perfect go-to. Sitting in silence and emptying the mind of thought is amazing. When you add mindful breathing as a focus tool, you have a calm-the-heck-down exercise that can be done anywhere—at home, in your car, or even in the office bathroom because Sally *really* pushed your buttons and you want to rip her a new one, but you won't because you're not a Bad Boss. With practice, stilling your mind can allow you to watch your thoughts skitter by like ants in the grass; rather than needing to chase them down, you can simply observe them as they pass.

If you're a person who loves silence, you can try meditating on your own, or use the simple box-breathing practice below. This is a great way to get centered before a big meeting or a challenging conversation, as you can do it anywhere and it takes less than two minutes.

Close your eyes or soften your gaze. Take a big breath in, and forcefully exhale. Do that again. Now, imagine your breath is drawing the shape of a box (or a square): As you breathe in for four counts, your breath draws one side of the square. Hold the breath for four counts as you draw the next side of the square. Then, exhale for four counts and draw another side. Finally, pause for four counts while your lungs are empty.

Inhale, 2, 3, 4. Hold, 2, 3, 4. Exhale 2, 3, 4. Pause, 2, 3, 4.

Repeat this at least ten times. When you're finished, slowly blink your eyes open and breathe normally. You may feel the need to pandiculate (that's a fifty-dollar word that means "to stretch involuntary") to get your blood flowing and muscles moving, and you'll notice that you feel relaxed and clear.

Another quick breathing technique is 4-6-4 breathing. Breathe in through your nose for a count of four, breathe out through pursed lips for a count of six, and pause on empty with lips closed for a count of four. Repeat at least five times.

You can also lean into guided meditations and visualizations. These are one of the most popular methods of centering and setting intentions. A gentle voice whisks your mind away to a place of serenity, providing calming instructions and positive affirmations to help you set intentions for the day and for the situation. You'll find several meditations to try at **www.unfunkyourselfbook.com**.

If sitting still and emptying your brain is challenging or frustrating even with guidance, mindful movement may be the way to go. Incorporating breathwork with mindful walking, simple yoga movements, and gentle stretches are excellent ways to get grounded so you can set mindful intentions and focus on what you really want from your day.

Journaling through writing or speaking helps our primal brain turn our worries into words, which are much easier to navigate than rogue thoughts that bounce around our brains. It can be helpful to keep a small notebook by your bed so you can jot down your thoughts in the morning or before bed. Or, if you prefer, you can use the voice memo app on your phone to speak your thoughts and reflections into a digital journal. Try replacing your usual nighttime social media doom-scrolling with ten minutes of journaling. Give yourself love for navigating your day and leaning into this mindful newness that will become your normal.

Again, there is no right way to focus and ground yourself, except the way that is right for you. All of these methods are valid and helpful, so find what works for you and go for it. What is most important is that you're doing it, and doing it often. I'm telling you, once you start weaving meditation, mindful movement, and/or journaling into your day, you will feel so much more calm, centered, and focused. Don't let it be intimidating; start slowly and build, like with any new habit.

COMMITMENT

Becoming a mindful leader (and human) doesn't happen overnight. Accept that you will get thrown off your game a bit. It happens. Don't judge it, just flow with it.

The reality of life is that we can set intentions, meditate, breathe, and move mindfully, and still tumble into a mindless moment when we deliver a bad presentation, are dealing with a hard deadline, are confronted by an irate coworker, or just get served really dreadful coffee. However, the more mindful you become, the more easily you can recalibrate and reset. The coffee issue might require antacids, but the others just need patience, breathing, and a moment of calm. Recognize what your body is telling you and honor its need for attention. Emotionally unsettling moments (those "Hot Zone moments") require attention and care. Your ego wants you to stay hot, but your body (and your team) needs you to cool down. Your body requires calm to function properly.

So, commit—not to perfection, but to the practice of mindfulness. Pause. Breathe. Assess. Reflect. Do it even (and especially) when you don't want to. With time, practice, and intention, you'll notice that you're less bothered by the little things, and that fewer moments of conflict arise in your day-to-day life. When you do get triggered, it will be easier to recognize and navigate.

Be POISED

As part of your commitment to be a more mindful leader, try being POISED in your day-to-day life.

Because I'm both fascinated and humbled by some of the awesome people I've been lucky enough to work with, I developed the POISED Method as a way to corral the mind-squirrels and keep myself grounded during speaking engagements, workshops, and difficult conversations.

POISED is an acronym that stands for Purpose, Objectivity, Integrity, Sincerity, Empathy, and Dialogue.

Let's break those down one by one.

Purpose

Eric expertly juggles numerous projects and manages a variety of engineers and project managers.

To lead his diverse team well, and to maintain an efficient, productive, and harmonious environment for them to succeed, Eric approaches conversations and meetings with purpose. He sets the intention of the conversation, clearly laying out his expectations for everyone involved, including himself, and aligns the discussion with both individual and team goals and objectives.

His direct reports and colleagues trust in Eric's ability to guide them. They know that meetings will be meaningful and that he will not waste their time or his own.

Objectivity

Peter has a keen ability to connect with everyone he encounters, even those with whom he doesn't initially resonate or even like. He understands that each of us is a product of our own experiences, and those experiences must be acknowledged and honored regardless of personal alignment.

He approaches conversations, even hard ones, with an open mind, acknowledging that he may not know all of the information. He keeps his biases in check and refrains from making assumptions; rather, he seeks each person's truth so that he can better understand them and adjust his approach and actions.

Integrity

Greg was a board member for an organization related to a profession to which he'd dedicated his entire career. As the organization expanded and the board of directors' membership shifted, he observed that the core values and mission of the organization were no longer at the forefront; rather, the egos of some of the new board members were now front and center.

Staying true to his convictions, he emphatically voiced his concerns, even in the face of adversity. Refusing to be shamed and staying true to his values, he did the right thing, even though it was hard, by stepping down from the board to focus his talents and energy on his business and with other organizations with whom he shared vision and values.

Sincerity

Offering expertise on communication, trust, inclusion, and belonging, Varsey is a ray of love in human form. Guided by her core values, she shows up authentically in conversations and interactions, modeling sincerity, quickly building trust, and demonstrating courage, honesty, and transparency. She exhibits humor, grace, and genuine care for others' needs and success.

Empathy

Erin runs a social services agency that serves a uniquely diverse population, many of whom are new Americans. Demonstrating true empathy, she does not view her clients through a lens of pity. Instead, she tunes in to their stories and feelings, ensuring that she can adjust her communication and service approach to fit their needs. This provides a generative experience for them, for her, and for the agency as a whole.

Dialogue

As an executive leader focused on lean processes and human efficiencies, Brian knows the importance of keeping his finger on the pulse of the firm's diverse employee base.

Approachable, responsive, and always respectful of his colleagues, he seeks "productive discord" by providing space for two-way conversations, especially when those conversations are challenging. Knowing that what's on the surface isn't the full truth, Brian excavates the roots of issues through open-ended questions and active listening.

***

As you prepare for meetings, evaluations, and conversations with employees—and even as you prepare for your workday—run through the POISED Method to-do list to help you begin and remain in a mindful space:

- Set the intention of this conversation
- Align discussion with goals and objectives
- Clearly lay out expectations
- Ditch the assumptions
- Check your biases
- Approach with an open mind
- Do the right thing
- Honor the mission
- Maintain alignment with values
- Be authentic
- Provide genuine care for success
- Be honest and transparent
- Attune to others' feelings
- Adjust communication to fit their needs
- Provide generative (not destructive) direction
- Give space for a two-way conversation
- Ask open-ended questions
- Seek productive discord

There is an inverse relationship between leading POISED and leading Funked-up. As you constantly commit to implementing intention into your conversations, meetings, and general existence in the workplace, you'll notice those funked-up behaviors start to dissipate.

Reflect Daily

Your commitment to being intentional requires being in tune with yourself. One effective way to tune in is to practice daily reflections.

At the end of your day, instead of scrolling mindlessly through socials, take a quiet moment to reflect on the intention that you set for your day and how that worked out. What went really well? What was funny? What was hard? What did you accomplish that you're proud of? What didn't go so well and how can you do better next time? What do you hope for tomorrow to be? What steps will you take to make that happen?

It's good to level-set with yourself, especially if you had some mindless moments throughout the day. You're human, it happens—and through consistent reflection, you will adjust and learn to flow.

HUMILITY

Humility and mindfulness go hand in hand.

Humility is an important leadership quality because it allows space for you to recognize your own strengths and importance without placing yourself above others. Really, humility is acknowledging that you're human, just like the people you're leading, and that you all have both flaws and limitations as well as excellent potential to learn and grow.

Humble leaders understand that everyone has value and that their worth is not tied to outward status or superiority. They know and feel that they are not just individuals, but also part of a larger whole.

Gratitude

Where and how we focus our energy matters greatly.

Let's do a quick exercise. Think of three aspects of your life for which you are truly grateful. Picture them clearly and really focus on the deep gratitude you feel for them. Do that for a few minutes. Just sit in gratitude for these aspects.

How do you feel? Jot down those thoughts in your journal or go to **www.unfunkyourselfbook.com** to download a handy gratitude journal.

Practicing gratitude can reduce anxiety and stress by triggering the brain to release neurotransmitters and hormones associated with happiness, including dopamine and serotonin. When we are happier, we are more tolerant, more productive, and calmer—all things that help us un-funk our approach to leading and living.

Don't Try to Be a Superstar

Some of us, when we decide to make mindfulness part of our leadership practice, decide that we are going to be the *best, most awesomely mindful* leader on the planet, starting *right now*, thank you very much.

How do you think that's going to work out, hmm?

Maybe about as well as that time you bought all the healthy veggies the grocery store had to offer because you decided you're going to eat healthy *all the time* from now until forever—and then, three weeks later, you opened the fridge and wondered what could have possibly died in there, only to discover that the stench is coming from a big, mushy bag of lettuce behind the can of whipped cream you bought to go with the double-chocolate ice cream you DoorDashed while bingeing *Bridgerton*.

Same, my friend. Same.

Creating habits can be hard. Breaking old habits is hard, too. And if you have habits that belong in the Funked-Up Boss category, don't expect to change them overnight.

When it comes to personal growth, humility is your friend.

Humans, as we've discussed, are funky by design, but we can un-funk ourselves by taking it one little bite-sized practice at a time. It's all about staying humble and taking baby steps. Trying to change too many rituals at one time ends up creating stress and makes the change unsustainable—hence the pint of double-chocolate ice cream.

So, try swapping out one mindless habit or ritual a month with one that is healthier or more mindful. For example, instead of scrolling socials in bed when you're supposed to be going to sleep—which, as we know from all sorts of research, leads to unhealthy brain stimulation and messes with our circadian rhythm—try reading an actual book in bed. Or replace one unhealthy snack in your lunchbox with something less unhealthy instead of restocking the whole fridge.

UN-FUNK YOUR DAYS

My favorite fitness trainer, Amoila Cesar, reminds us to *chop wood, carry water.* This phrase originates in Zen Buddhism and conveys the idea of finding meaning and mindfulness in everyday tasks, no matter how simple or mundane they may seem. It's a reminder to stay grounded, present, and focused on the basics of life, even as one progresses in personal, professional, and/or spiritual growth.

You've just read the literal manual on how to be a more mindful leader. Now, it's time to do it. Chop that wood. Carry that water. Be in the action of mindfulness.

Showing up more mindfully is going to be weird at first, and you might feel strange or silly. But strange and silly are far better than funked up! Just keep going. And, if you work with people who are a little bit funked up also, share this book with them so they can chop and carry and try and grow, too.

I believe in you. Now you go on and believe in you, too.

Namaste, friends.
Emily

RESOURCES

Download all the resources and meditations mentioned in this book at **www.unfunkyourselfbook.com**.

Take the Communication Compass assessment FREE at **www.unfunkyourselfbook.com**.

Want Emily to help you Un-Funk your leadership team? Reach out to **hamptonmorashllc@gmail.com** to inquire about workshops, trainings, keynotes, and private coaching.

ACKNOWLEDGMENTS

THIS BOOK WOULD NOT have been possible without the love, support, and persistent nudges from my incredibly patient and caring husband, Don. You are my rock, my puzzle piece, my lobster. I love you more. Thank you for believing in me.

Thank you also to ...

My children, Kory, Emily, Luke, and Colin, who inspire me to make the world a better place for them and their children (should they ever choose to have them). This book is the best way I know how to do that. I hope I make them as proud as they make me.

My mom, Pat, a composed and meticulous journalist, who taught me how to write and also how to negotiate, and who emphasized the importance of relentlessly pursuing the roots and reasons behind every story.

My dad, David, who imparted to me his love of football (Go Vols!), the importance of keeping the faith, and the joy of gathering and sharing obscure knowledge.

My sister, Nicole, a clever, hilarious, and resilient role model with an incredibly beautiful soul, for her unwavering patience, protection, love, and support, and the most wonderful "seester" adventures ever. You're more important to me than you know.

My long-time friend Scott, (without whom I would never have met Bryna, my fascinating and ever-patient publisher), for being a steadfast, ever-silly friend, always holding space for me, and offering kindness and grace as I tumbled down the rabbit hole of that massive life upheaval.

Bryna, my magical editor and publisher, who provided direction, hope, humor, and space. I am so grateful to have met you. And now you're stuck with me.

Gage Greenwood, sweet friend and horror writer extraordinaire, who, through his raw honesty and humanness, inspired me to create this book and write what I knew needed to be shared. Your presence in my life is a gift.

My lifeline friend group: Heidi Swanson, Amy Gorman, Allary Litherland, Jason Houck, Patrick Tiller, Rebecca Stockdill, Patty Wind, Ann Katz, Laura Shady, Dawn Ragle, and Sean O'Hearne, who, whether they know it or not, lifted me up during this exciting and challenging process, and believed in me even when I didn't.

And finally, my clients and colleagues who allowed me to include their stories in the book. I've learned as much from you as you've learned from me, and I am forever grateful for your trust.

ABOUT THE AUTHOR

AFTER TWO INSPIRATIONAL and successful decades in nonprofit development and leadership, Emily Hampton Morash shifted her focus, founding Hampton Morash, LLC to address the pressing issues she observed during her tenure in the community-based and corporate nonprofit world.

Recognizing the prevalence of disharmonious workplace cultures, leadership skills gaps, team cohesion needs, and an overall misunderstanding of productive communication, she certified for and developed robust and immediately applicable targeted curricula.

Her professional experience and education provide a solid skill set, including exceptional workshop facilitation, training impact, and coaching connection. Presenting with a dynamic and engaging energy, she fosters proactive, layered, exploratory conversations sprinkled with humor, insight, and discovery.

Emily teaches graduate and undergraduate courses for Johnson and Wales University. She is also a lead instructor for the Accelerated Training Center for Workforce Development at Columbus State Community College and has instructed workforce development and leadership development classes for the Community College of Rhode Island and Bryant University.

Emily received a B.A. in Sociology from the University of Tennessee and earned her M.S. in Community Economic Development from Southern New Hampshire University. She is a certified mediator, Mindfulness, Confidence, and REBT coach, Everything DiSC® certified partner, Five Behaviors™ certified partner, and the creator of The Communication Compass™, The Mindful Leader Practice™, and the Origins of Identity Practice™. She is a professional facilitator, public speaker, leadership and career coach—and now an author.

Emily lives in Ohio with her two younger children, her husband Don, two dogs, three cats, and the squirrels in her head. When she's not leading workshops, classes, and trainings, you can find her hanging out at home, in her garden, or meandering through a bookstore. She spends a silly amount of time scouring the interwebs in search of concert tickets and cool music festivals.

Learn more about Emily at **www.hamptonmorash.com**.

ABOUT THE PUBLISHER

FOUNDED IN 2021 by Bryna Haynes, WorldChangers Media is a boutique publishing company focused on "Ideas for Impact."

We know that great books can change lives, topple outdated paradigms, and build movements. Our commitment is to deliver superior-quality transformational nonfiction by, and for, the next generation of thought leaders, conscious entrepreneurs, creatives, healers, and industry disruptors.

Ready to write and publish your thought leadership book with us? Learn more at **www.WorldChangers.Media**.

WORLDCHANGERS
MEDIA